SAVAGE SLAUGHTER

Barbara Muszalski didn't realize the depth of ranch hand Robert Gonzales's obsession with her. As soon as he climbed into her Chevy pickup, he again insisted that she go with him to New York or Los Angeles. She told him to stop.

Gonzales pulled a stolen ten-inch butcher knife out of his jacket and stabbed Muszalski. She threw up her arm to deflect the next blow, but her efforts were in vain. In a blur of unleashed frenzy, he cut into her arms, then into her hands, slashing so viciously that the tendons were cut down to the bone. He moved on to her torso, deeply stabbing her breasts and abdomen, before slashing her face three times. His final blow to her chest was so savage that it sliced through her aorta and broke off a piece of the knife handle.

Gonzales's rage was spent. He'd stabbed Muszalski twenty-two times, leaving her slaughtered and the inside of her pickup's cab and himself sprayed with blood and gore.

SAVAGE

Robert Scott

PINNACLE BOOKS
Kensington Publishing Corp.
http://www.kensingtonbooks.com

Some names have been changed to protect the privacy of individuals connected to this story.

PINNACLE BOOKS are published by

Kensington Publishing Corp.
850 Third Avenue
New York, NY 10022

Copyright © 2002 by Robert Scott

ABERDEENSHIRE LIBRARY AND INFORMATION SERVICES	
2572262	
HJ	530053
364.152	£5.99
	ANF

buted Lines are
bulk purchases
ng, and educa-
rpts or custom-
cific needs. For
details, write or phone the office of the Kensington special sales manager: Kensington Publishing Corp., 850 Third Avenue, New York, NY 10022, attn: Special Sales Department, Phone: 1-800-221-2647.

Pinnacle and the P logo Reg. U.S. Pat. & TM Off.

First Printing: April 2002
10 9 8 7 6 5 4 3 2

Printed in the United States of America

ACKNOWLEDGMENTS

Many people helped in the preparation of this book. I'd particularly like to thank Nancy Ballard, Dave Holbrook, former NYPD Detective Mike Geddes, Alameda County Inspector Brian Lerche, Sheriff's Lieutenant Dale Toussaint, Inspector Kathy Boyovich, and LAPD Detective Frank Bolan. I'd also like to thank my terrific literary agent, Damaris Rowland, and my wonderful editor at Pinnacle Books, Karen Haas.

"Benjamin Gonzales is the single most dangerous individual presently housed in the Alameda County Jail and he will certainly be among the most dangerous inmates to be housed anywhere in the California State Prison System . . . I have never come in contact with any person whom I believe embodies the traits of sadistic brutality, viciousness, lack of remorse and depravity to the degree these traits are exhibited in Mr. Gonzales."

—Alameda County Superior Court Judge Jeffrey Horner

I

THE CHAMELEON

One

Other Side of the
Magic Kingdom

Los Angeles, California
Saturday, February 4, 1989—6:20 A.M.

Mrs. Ellen Blake couldn't sleep, so she got up early to face another cool, but pleasant, southern California winter morning. Even though it was February, the day promised to be seventy-eight degrees later on in the afternoon. She lived in a quiet residential neighborhood on Victoria Avenue in an area of older bungalows and stucco homes. Just an ordinary neighborhood now, these had been elegant homes in the 1920's. Buster Keaton had once lived up the street on Victoria Avenue and had even filmed the block in his movie *Seven Chances*. In one unforgettable scene, he was chased by hundreds of frantic prospective brides as he ran down the street.

Some of the houses were a little worse for

wear now, but the palm trees lining the street
still gave the district an exotic air. Mrs. Blake
was just putting the coffee on when she heard
a car door slam out on the street, followed
shortly thereafter by the distinct smell of
smoke. She peeked out her front window and
was startled to see a car across the street starting to erupt into flames. Astonished by the
sight, she dashed to her telephone and dialed
911.

Within minutes, a fire engine from the local
firehouse arrived on the scene to battle the
blaze that now fully engulfed the vehicle. The
crew of firemen surrounded the car and sprayed
a stream of special retardant on the fire until it
was fully out. Only after it had cooled a bit and
was safe did one of the firemen peek in the window of the 1977 Pontiac Trans Am. He'd seen
many things in his time, but what he witnessed
now made him rock back in horror. Propped
up on the front seat behind the steering wheel
was the still smouldering body of a young
woman. She may have been beautiful once, but
all that was left of her now was a charred carcass
and the sickening smell of burnt flesh. Her face
was blackened beyond recognition by the fire
until it hardly looked human. Everything in the
vehicle had been burned completely except for
a few schoolbooks, a fanny pack and one more
chilling item. Lying on the floorboard was a
double-edged palm dagger.

No doubt about it, Dondi Johnson was a very
lovely young woman. Twenty-two years old in

1989, she grew up in the fabled land of southern California. Santa Monica and Redondo Beaches were to the west, Hollywood to the north up the Golden State Freeway, and Disneyland lay just to the south down the Santa Ana Freeway. It was still a land of make-believe, where dreams came true on the silver screen. The bronze stars on the Hollywood walk of fame, only a few miles away, attested to that. Celebrities really did live up in the hills of Brentwood and Beverly Hills, and beachboys and girls did frolic in the surf down at Malibu and Huntington Beach. The temperatures in winter were always warm and sometimes the song seemed true that proclaimed, "It never rains in southern California."

But Dondi Johnson lived somewhere on the other side of the Magic Kingdom. Her neighborhood was no longer a dreamland or a theme park. By the 1980's, there were more gang-bangers than orange groves in the "hood." Every corner seemed to hold either a drug addict or a prostitute. Even friendly and outgoing Dondi Johnson had been touched by all the chaos. She was a single unwed mother by the time she was twenty years old, and could have easily fallen into the malaise that so many young women of her neighborhood were prone to. But she was also a go-getter, and by the late 1980's, she'd turned her life around and was attending Cerritos College full-time to better her future. She wanted a better life not only for herself, but her child as well. She took the regular courses for a general education de-

gree, as well as theater and dance classes. In
her pursuit, she spread a kind of warmth and
natural charm around her. She was so well-
liked that fellow students in January 1989
elected her to the student senate. Cerritos College, with its green lawns and safe buildings,
was like a haven of peace and calm compared
to where she'd grown up.

By now she lived in the city of Paramount
and even though it was only across the Los
Angeles River from where she had grown up,
the river was a psychological as well as physical
dividing line. Things were safer there and
more upscale. Dondi Johnson by 1989 seemed
like a young woman on the rise.

There was only one thing wrong to darken
the horizon—a nagging worry about money.
Tuition and books were expensive, to say nothing of the bills she had to pay for ordinary
living expenses. To make ends meet, she took
a job as a "chip girl" at a card room in Bell
Gardens called the Bicycle Club. Her duties
weren't really onerous; they merely entailed
handing out chips to the bettors in the card
room. But the hours were long when added to
the classes, homework and daily chores.

The Bicycle Club wasn't some dingy, hole-in-
the-wall card room. Built like a modern Las
Vegas casino, it could hold nearly 2,000 people
in its main card room. Chandeliers decorated
the ceiling, and restaurants, bars, and even a
hair salon graced the hallways. On the main
floor, a bettor had a choice of playing Hi-Lo,
California Poker, Mexican Poker, Pan and half

a dozen other card games. The clientele was a cross-section of Los Angeles population; whites, blacks, Hispanics and Asians all rubbed elbows at the Bicycle Club, waiting for fortune to turn their way. Earnest gamblers leaned over their cards, hoping for that one chance that was going to change everything in their lives.

Dondi Johnson fit right into the upscale establishment with her pleasant looks and friendly nature. She became just as popular with the patrons of the Bicycle Club as the students of Cerritos College.

One employee of the club in particular, named James Angel, was especially taken with her. He was a handsome young Hispanic man with curly dark hair, expressive brown eyes and a well-built 180-pound frame. He liked to keep himself in shape. It helped with the line of work he was in. He was a bodyguard/enforcer/money collector for a local Asian street gang. His main job was to collect loan shark debts that were owed by customers who frequented the Pai Gow Parlor in the back of the Bicycle Club. Even though the Bicycle Club did not condone loansharking activity, it was common around all card rooms in the state.

The Pai Gow Parlor was a smaller version of the main card room, but it was no less elegant. A potential bettor passed through a marble foyer with waterfalls running down rough-hewn granite walls. The room had an Asian motif and was always crowded.

Pai Gow, a game popular with many Asians in the area, was played with thirty-two domino-like tiles that were shuffled by the dealer and then put into eight stacks of four. The bettors placed their money directly in front of a pile. Then the dealer shook dice in a cup to determine which stack would go to which player. Finally, the bettors divided their tiles into two groups—a high hand and low hand. A lot of money could be lost or won playing Pai Gow. More than one bettor got in over his head and lost more than he could afford. That was where the loan sharks came in, offering more quick money at exorbitant interest rates. That was where James Angel came in, as well. His job was to "persuade" reluctant debtors to pay up on time.

Despite the rough nature of his craft, Angel was soft-spoken and quiet. Dondi Johnson found him both charming and a little bit shy. She enjoyed his polite attentions and almost-chivalrous style. She didn't even mind that he sometimes went by other names for some obscure reason. He sometimes called himself "Nick D'Amico" or just "Ben." In some ways it added to his air of mystery. There was only one problem: Dondi already had a boyfriend named Marvin Byers. He was helping her get out of the hole she had dug for herself. Even though she occasionally had a drink with James Angel, or shared a meal with him at the restaurant, it was nothing more than a friendly gesture on her part.

The same could not be said for Angel. What started out as an infatuation soon turned into a downright obsession. He couldn't take his eyes off Johnson as she moved around the club. His thoughts kept returning to her again and again. He began following her everywhere around the card room as she passed out chips. It got to the point that it was interfering with her job.

He not only fantasized about Dondi Johnson, but as 1988 turned into 1989, he began to ask her to move away from Los Angeles with him. He said they could have a better life together. He stressed that Marvin Byers wasn't the right man for her. Only Angel was.

Johnson began to become concerned at his constant attention and flights of fantasy. It was obvious to her by now that what was only a casual relationship to her, had become much more than that in James's mind. He mistook her naturally friendly ways for a mutual bond of deep affection. She eventually told Marvin Byers about it and said that something had to be done.

On the evening of February 3, 1989, James Angel phoned Johnson at her residence and pleaded with her once again, "You've got to move to New York with me!"

She hung up on him instead. When Byers asked who had phoned, she said angrily, "It was James. I told him to buzz off!"

The next day at the Bicycle Club, James Angel was even more insistent. Though Dondi Johnson tried to avoid him, he managed to corner her and again pleaded, "I want you to marry me and move to New York. You've got forty-eight hours to decide." He then pulled

three one-hundred-dollar bills out of his wallet
for airline tickets to prove he was serious.

Dondi told him to shut up and leave her
alone.

What happened next comes in two versions,
depending on who witnessed it. One person
said he saw Dondi Johnson tear up the hun-
dred-dollar bills and sprinkle their remains on
the floor in front of Angel. The other version
is even more chilling. According to that witness, James Angel pulled out a cigarette lighter
and set fire to the bills. Then he swore, "This
is what's going to happen to you."

Dondi Johnson now knew that he was not
only obsessed, but crazy as well.

She should have avoided him completely after that, but for some inexplicable reason,
Dondi agreed to give him a ride home after
her shift was over. Perhaps she was just too
good-hearted to hold a grudge for long. Or
maybe he was convincingly apologetic. For
whatever reason, Johnson and Angel climbed
into her 1977 Trans Am about five A.M. on February 4, 1989, and headed for the quiet residential neighborhood of Victoria Avenue clear
across town in the direction of Hollywood.

When they arrived, Angel started in on his
obsessive behavior once again. Thoroughly sick
of it, Johnson told him to go to hell. He did.
In a blinding fury, he pulled out a double-
edged dagger with a palm handle. She threw
up her hand to ward off the blow, but he cut
right through it down to the bone. He slashed
her arm, her face, her neck and her breasts.

The blade sliced into her chest and abdomen. He was absolutely fixated on stabbing her upper body, especially her face. He made sure he stabbed her in the eye. Then he stabbed her so deeply in the chest that it severed her aorta. He made a savage blow into her midsection and pulled upward in a final horrifying coup de grace. Everything was splattered with blood. James Angel just didn't stab Dondi Johnson; he slaughtered her. By the time his fury was through, almost every square inch of the front seat of the Trans Am was splattered with blood, and so was he.

Panting and out of breath after his rage subsided, he suddenly realized he had to get out of there. He quietly opened the passenger door and then crept away up the still quiet street.

Attorney William McKinney was sound asleep on Saturday morning at his residence on Victoria Place, just around the corner from the murder scene, when he heard a knock at his front door. Dazed and tired, he wondered what time it was. He looked at the bedroom clock and was surprised to see that it was only about six A.M. Hoping the person would just go away proved to be futile. The intruder kept knocking at the door. Grumbling, McKinney got out of bed, answered the front door and was startled to see one of his former clients standing there. It was James Angel and his clothes were covered with blood.

McKinney knew James Angel both professionally and socially. He had represented him years before in Los Angeles. In fact, after that trial, Angel and McKinney had become friends. Angel often called his old attorney and even dropped by his house on occasion. At one point, he helped move new furniture into McKinney's home and took some of the old furniture in return.

McKinney was also aware that James Angel often used the name Ben, and that recently he had been talking about a woman named Dondi all the time. He had told McKinney, "I'm very much in love with her. She's my girlfriend." James Angel had talked about Dondi every time they met and had even reportedly brought her by the house one time. He seemed to be very enamored of her. But McKinney knew that Angel tended to be obsessive about people and things. As far as Dondi went, he seemed to have an incredible fixation on her.

Now here was James Angel standing at his front door, covered in blood and claiming lamely that he had been "jumped" by a couple of guys. McKinney was suspicious of this story immediately. James was not only covered with blood, but he had a deep cut on one of his fingers and another behind one ear. The attorney wondered how anyone could get cut behind the ear.

Nonetheless McKinney invited him in and suggested that Angel change his clothes. They were about the same height and weight at the time and Angel accepted a pair of pants and a shirt. McKinney's wife came downstairs and handed McKinney some towels, which he applied to James's wounds to stop the bleeding.

James Angel was grateful for the attention, but he was also nervous. His agitation grew even stronger when he said, "I lost my wallet somewhere. I'll be back."

Angel was gone for nearly fifteen minutes and it was starting to get light outside by the time he returned. Even more agitated now, he said that he had not found his wallet.

In fact, he had returned to the scene of the crime and, not finding his wallet, he had quickly struck on a plan to destroy as much evidence as he could. He built a small pyramid of items in the car next to Dondi Johnson's slaughtered body, and set them all afire. Then he quickly left the area and returned to William McKinney's house.

Knowing now that the authorities would soon be on their way to the car fire, Angel begged McKinney for a ride to his apartment in Hollywood, about five miles away. McKinney was not thrilled by this prospect, but agreed. As they both got into McKinney's car, Angel suddenly made an unusual request. He asked that McKinney drive the long way to Venice Boulevard. The normal route would have been to turn the corner onto the 1400 block of Victoria Avenue and then to Venice Boulevard. James Angel was adamant about this new route, and McKinney was in no mood to argue with him. They turned left instead of right, away from the 1400 block of Victoria Avenue.

As they drove along, McKinney noticed that Angel had bundled up his bloody clothing and was carrying it with him, along with the bloody towel. As they neared Hollywood, Angel asked, "If I'm in trouble, will you help me?"

McKinney said that he would.

James Angel blurted out, "I just killed my girlfriend."

McKinney was stunned and placed in a no-win situation. What he had just heard was covered under attorney-client privilege. It was the same as someone confessing to a priest or a spouse. The receiving party of this information could not be compelled to tell authorities what they had just heard. Morally, McKinney was obligated to do something. But legally, he could not. Besides, he knew that James often exaggerated the facts. Maybe he was doing the same once again.

While he pondered what to do about the situation, McKinney dropped Angel off on Yucca Street in Hollywood, and then returned toward his home on Victoria Place. It was about six-thirty A.M. by now. As he drove past the 1400 block of Victoria Avenue, he was startled to see fire trucks, a smouldering car by the curb and lots of law enforcement personnel milling around behind yellow police tape cordoning off the area. It wasn't hard to put two and two together. William McKinney wasn't sure what James Angel had done at that point, but he was sure it was pretty bad. That he had indeed "killed his girlfriend" was a distinct possibility.

Meanwhile, James Angel grabbed a few items of clothing from his apartment, stuffed them into a duffel bag, and just as the sun was starting to shine on the famous Hollywood sign in the hills, he walked down the street, turned a corner and disappeared from the streets of Los Angeles.

Two

Show World

Mike Geddes of the New York Police Department had no illusions about just how tough the Big Apple could be. He had started out as a rookie in 1973 in the 83rd Precinct. It was a high-crime area and he learned how to take care of himself and his partner on foot patrols, police car patrols and eventually in the anti-crime plainclothes unit. In 1982, he transferred to the Organized Crime Control Bureau and was assigned to the Brooklyn North Narcotics Unit. The scenery was different, but just as dangerous. After years of battling narcotics, he earned his detective's badge in 1985.

By 1987, he was transferred again to the epitome of New York City's police detail—the Midtown South Detective Unit that covered the area of Times Square. It was heady stuff being right in the middle of all the action. Here even crime didn't take a holiday. The whole area was a haven for dangerous criminals and lunatics. In the very heart of this district was an

adult entertainment venue called the Show
World Theater. Detective Geddes recalled just
what a crazy scene it was there as the new de-
cade of the 1990's began.

"The area around the Show World Theater
at Forty-second Street and Eighth Avenue was
called 'The Deuce' by the people who lived
there," he said. "It was an area full of bright
lights and people always milling around. The
Port Authority Bus Terminal was located right
across the street and this brought lots of people in from the suburbs. But even more than
this, it was a haven for runaways coming in
from the rest of the states. There were lots of
drug dealers, prostitutes, transvestites and XXX
movie houses in the area. It was a fast lane
type of locale; always something happening.
Thousands of working people moved through
the area quickly to get to their trains and buses
to take them to and from work. The rest of
the time it was taken over by con games, drugs,
sex and robbery. The New Yorkers were always
aware of the bad guys in the area and moved
on. But the outsiders and weak persons were
easy marks.

"There was lots of homeless people there in
1991. They lived around the Port Authority in
boxes. They actually set up a box city. About
a block away, the boxes were so big, they called
them condos. These were big refrigerator
boxes where they lived, cooked, had sex and
did drugs. These homeless people would hang
out in the Show World area and solicit sex
from the patrons. It was a regular zoo around

there. Tourists would drop by just to see all the crazy stuff going on."

Detective Geddes not only knew The Deuce well, but knew what went on inside the Show World Theater as well. He said, "Show World was a place where young girls from all backgrounds came to work as dancers on stages. Some of the stages were surrounded by small booths where guys would pay a quarter to peep into the show. Some of the girls were college girls trying to make some extra money. Others were drug addicts and prostitutes. Men would come in there from all working classes, day or night. There were rich, poor, professionals, tourists, married men, you name it. There were XXX movies to watch, the girls taking off their clothes and dancing around, and even though they won't admit it, sex all over the place in that theater."

One of the dancers in the Show World Theater was a girl named Yvonne Hausley. Just like Detective Mike Geddes, Yvonne had no illusions about the Big Apple. New York City to her was gritty and rough, and Yvonne learned to adapt and grow tough just to survive. Some thought she came from a small town in New Jersey, but whatever her origin, she was a big-city girl now. The same age as Dondi Johnson had been in 1989, there were no palm trees or sunny beaches for her. She plunged into the depths of the concrete-and-steel canyons of Manhattan to find her way in life. Like Dondi

Johnson, however, Yvonne Hausley was a college girl and a good student. She also had a child who was seven years old. Hausley had been living with a New York City policeman for four years and had stabilized the rougher edges of her life. But just like Dondi Johnson, she needed extra money to help pay for college expenses. She had a nice face and body and knew what men liked. She decided at a young age to use her "assets" to advantage. She became an exotic dancer at strip clubs in the New York area.

By 1991, she'd worked her way up to Show World in the very heart of Manhattan. While working there, she bumped and shimmied to the pounding music, fulfilling the patron's sexual fantasies in the darkened interior. Yvonne Hausley was no fool, and she gave the customers what they wanted. Dancing up close to eager men of all ages, she willingly accepted the money they passed to her or laid on the corner of the stage in appreciation of her performances.

Also in 1991, a new employee, who called himself Antonio Perillo, came to work at Show World. He was a handsome young Hispanic man with curly dark hair, expressive brown eyes and a well-built 180-pound frame. He became a coin clerk at Show World. Patrons would hand him money and he would give them tokens in return to use at the porno video machines in the booths set along one wall. Though he was quiet spoken and kind of cute in Yvonne Hausley's estimation, she was living with a policeman at the time. But this didn't keep her from flirting with him in a casual way. She would have a bite to eat with him once in a while, or talk with him in the hallway. It was nothing serious, just something to pass the time and make the hours move more quickly between her acts on stage.

As the months passed, she thought it was kind of amusing to see the way he got so worked up about her. He was a prime example of what fools men could be in the presence of a pretty woman. She teased him innocently, just to see how flustered he would get. But what was no more than a game to her became a downright obsession with Antonio. He followed her around the theater everywhere she went, finding excuses just to be by her side. After a while, he didn't even look at the other girls. His attentions were focused solely upon Yvonne Hausley. He constantly offered to buy her meals and to give her money. Even though cash was always welcome, she began to turn him down because he was so persistent. The result turned him into a pouting little boy.

If some of the other men in the audience had "crushes" on her, these were nothing compared to the ridiculous extremes that Perillo was taking their so-called "relationship." He acted like some nerdy teenage boy who had the hots for the local beautiful cheerleader.

Steven Conroy, a cashier and manager on the second floor, was well aware of Perillo's obsession with Hausley. He commented, "Tony would offer Yvonne food, offer to take her to lunch, to dinner, to the movies. Yvonne would say no. She had a boyfriend."

By February 1991, Hausley started treating Antonio Perillo more like the joke he had become, than a friend—egging him on in his wild fantasies. Perillo became so upset by this behavior that he told another employee at Show World, "She's broken up with me so she can have a lesbo affair with one of the other dancers." In point of fact, she had never "been" with him in the first place, nor was she a lesbian. The whole idea of them being a couple was a figment of his wild imagination.

A few weeks later, he told another employee, "If I can't have Yvonne, no one can. She's been sleeping with the manager and a cop. She's fucking with my head. Don't be surprised if you see me in the papers for killing her!"

By the third week of March 1991, Antonio Perillo was a truly pathetic individual as he followed Yvonne Hausley around in the semidark interior of Show World while music pounded in the background and girls slowly took off their clothing on stage. He offered her meals, flowers and money, all of which she now totally refused. It sent him into a frenzy like a manic wind-up toy. He begged her to move away with him to somewhere far beyond the walls of Show World. He'd take care of her, he said. She wouldn't have to strip in front of ogling men for a living.

Yvonne Hausley just laughed at him.

* * *

Around twelve-thirty P.M. on Sunday, March 21, 1991, Yvonne Hausley came into the theater wearing street clothes and Steven Conroy assigned her to the Triple Treat Theater section of Show World. She changed into revealing silky lingerie in one of the booths, but before she could take her assigned place, Antonio Perillo came up to her in the hallway, as needy as ever.

Conroy heard Perillo say to her, "I'd like to speak with you. Let's go into this section where it's a lot quieter."

Perillo pointed toward an area behind a closed door called the Big Top Lounge. It was a bar that was under construction and no one was in there on that Sunday afternoon.

Surprisingly, Hausley followed Perillo into the lounge, and Conroy lost sight of them behind the bar's door.

Once inside, Perillo begged her one more time to move away with him. He was absolutely desperate now. Her laughter and scorn rang in his ears and cut him to the quick. In an instant, he flew into a rage and became determined to cut her just as deeply. He pulled out a 007 Commando knife, while his free hand flew over her mouth. Then he slashed her face, her hands, her arms and her breasts. Against all her wild struggling, his strength was just too much. The sharp knife plunged into her chest and abdomen—one cut was so deep that it perforated her stomach and eviscerated her bowel. He stabbed right up her body in manic strokes until he reached her face again. He slashed her neck until the wounds cut right down to the spinal cord. The knife left a jagged gash in her neck. The blade plunged through her right eye and entered the brain. It was such a savage blow it nearly gouged her eye completely out of the socket. Then he stabbed her in her midsection with a savage thrust that ripped right up to the area of her heart.

By the time he was through, Antonio Perillo had stabbed her twenty-eight times, leaving an immense pool of blood on the floor. He dropped her slaughtered body onto the bloody floor and stalked out the door.

Realizing he had to create a diversion to keep everyone away from the backroom, Perillo walked up in full view of another employee and said, "I'm quitting!" He grabbed a handful of cash out of the register and ran out the front door.

But he wasn't quite through with Show World just yet. At four P.M. he phoned the manager from a pay phone and apologized for stealing the money. He said he'd be back with it in a couple of hours. The manager waited for him, but to no avail. Perillo had no intention of returning.

He went back to his place, packed a couple of small bags and showed up on the doorstep of a friend's house asking for money. The friend was the son of a rival "strip joint" owner, and he liked Perillo. He gave him some cash for a cab ride to the bus station and some extra money as well. One thing the friend noticed was a large fresh scratch mark on Perillo's face. He wondered how it had gotten there.

It wasn't until 8:50 P.M. that evening that a Show World employee needed to use a restroom and decided to go to the one in the back of the Big Top Lounge. Switching on a light, he suddenly spied something strange on the floor. It took a few moments to realize what his eyes were taking in. When he did, he yelled in horror. Lying in an immense pool of blood was the butchered body of Yvonne Hausley.

Meanwhile, Antonio Perillo had made his way down to the Port Authority Bus Terminal and climbed aboard an outbound bus. Then he simply disappeared.

Three

East of Eden

In the early 1980's, Barbara Muszalski found a little bit of Eden just to the east of the California town of Livermore. With her husband, Jim, a Silicon Valley sales manager, she bought a small ranch on Tesla Road in this pastoral enclave near the Altamont Hills. A lifelong enthusiast of ranching and farm life, she had finally fulfilled her dream of becoming a ranch wife with her own little spread. She had a natural gift with animals and soon became an expert in the field of dairy goat raising. Her seven-acre ranch included a four-bedroom, three-bath house, a 3,000-square-foot combination garage and barn, and extensive goat pens nestled atop a rise looking down upon the world-class vineyards of the Concannon and Wente Brothers wineries.

By 1991, Barbara had several turkeys, a few pigs and eighty goats on the Muszalski ranch. She did all the work with the animals—feeding them, doing the milking and cleaning out the barn. She got so proficient at her task that she even did all the veterinary work as well. Mary Gilman, a rancher from Los Altos, said of her, "She's extremely knowledgable about ranch animals. I'd always call Barb before I'd call a vet. She found lots of innovative ways of making her own cheese as well as raising pigs and turkeys."

Jim Muszalski pretty much left the running of the ranch to Barbara while he hopped on his motorcycle at seven-thirty A.M. each workday morning for the forty-mile ride to the Xerox Company in Silicon Valley. He was happy to leave her in her element while he delved into the world of computers and technology. She not only loved what she was doing, but loved sharing it with others as well. Barbara Muszalski helped with the local 4-H club and was always throwing barbecues and supper parties for neighbors. Neighbor and friend Jan Gonzalez remembered, "She was always joking and cutting up. You couldn't leave the house without your face hurting, you'd be laughing so hard. . . . And her famous dinners—she made homemade tempura along with homemade wine. A lot of times she forgot to eat herself, she was so busy getting people more shrimp tempura and fresh-ground horseradish."

Barbara Muszalski had a penchant for helping others. She took a troubled teenager, Robin Callahan, under her wing and gave her some direction. As Robin remembered, "I was fourteen years old, and my first love in life was animals. I wanted to raise dairy goats for show, and I bought my first two goats from Barbara. Our relationship grew from there. Within months, she had opened her heart and home to me. The whole family did. I became just as much a part of the family as anyone else. At that time I was going through my difficult teen-age years with my family and so spent most weekends, holidays and summers with Barbara and her family. Barbara became my best friend, my mentor and my mom. She taught me about goat raising, people, open-mindedness, rela-tionships, honesty, cooking, friendship, trust-ing, but most of all love. Jim and Barbara were always so sweet and kind to one another, hugs and kisses and pats. When I was there, I re-ceived more attention than ever. Everyone seemed pleased to have me, even if only four days had gone by. I was like a little angel there. Don't get me wrong. I did chores, and I helped out a hundred percent. I was not spoiled.

"Barbara had more friends than most people have in ten lifetimes. Everyone loved her. She had open house at Christmas and always a houseful. She also had an annual barbecue in the summer, and at Thanksgiving. The whole Muszalski family went and helped serve meals to the less fortunate. She was my life for nine years, and I can't recall anyone ever saying any-thing negative about her."

It was quite obvious by the summer of 1991 that Barbara Muszalski loved her ranch and loved life. Even though her four children were all grown up and out on their own, she found a dozen ways to keep herself happily busy. There were always new things to learn about dairy goat raising, and she loved sharing what she learned with others. One of the people she shared this with was Dave Williams, who owned a small ranch about two miles away on Lupin Way.

Dave Williams not only had a full-time job as manager of Rossi and Rivetti Flowers in San Francisco, but he raised dairy goats as well on his small Livermore ranch. Nestled beneath the Altamont Hills on rural Lupin Way, the ranch had a strange neighbor just across Greenville Road to the west—the Lawrence Livermore National Laboratories. This extensive military-industrial complex spread for miles over the terrain and dealt with not only nuclear weapons, but *"Star Wars"* technology as well. Built in 1952 as a response to the Soviet Union exploding a hydrogen bomb, the Livermore Lab by the 1990's employed thousands of people and had some of the top scientists in the land working there.

But on Dave Williams's side of Greenville Road, not much had changed since the Spanish land grant days. It was still a land of ranches and vineyards. Just like Barbara Muszalski, Dave Williams loved ranch life and animals. Before moving to Livermore, he had owned a dog kennel in beautiful Monterey, California. One day in 1980, a handsome young Hispanic man named Robert Gonzales, who weighed about 180 pounds and had expressive brown eyes, came by the kennel and asked for a job. Gonzales worked for Williams's half brother in San Jose, and he'd heard that Dave might need some help. Dave Williams put him to work mending some of the kennels and the young man was a whizz. There seemed to be nothing he couldn't do with a saw and hammer. Williams was so impressed by Gonzales's handiwork that he wanted to keep him on full time. But in a few days Robert Gonzales was gone just as quickly as he had arrived.

Out of the blue in June 1991, Dave Williams got a phone call from Robert Gonzales asking if he was the same person who had once owned a dog kennel in Monterey. When Williams said, "Yes," Gonzales asked if there were any jobs to do on the Williams ranch. He didn't have to ask twice. Odd jobs were a dime a dozen on a ranch, and Williams was already busy with his full-time job at the flower store. Besides, he remembered how handy Robert Gonzales was with tools. "Sure, come on out and I can put you to work right away," he said.

Gonzales was calling from southern California at the time, so he flew up to the Oakland airport and Williams met him there. Gonzales looked a little bit older now and wore his dark hair in a ponytail beneath a baseball cap. But all in all he was still the same quiet and polite individual that Dave Williams had remembered from the Monterey days.

Robert Gonzales was only supposed to stay a few days out at the Williams ranch while he

got his feet on the ground. There were always
more odd jobs to do than Williams had time
for, so he made a bargain with Robert Gonzales—he could stay in one of the back bed-
rooms of the house in exchange for work.
Williams would even throw in twenty dollars a
week of spending money. Gonzales agreed to
the deal and soon became a fixture at the Williams ranch.

Gonzales was not only good at carpentry, but
good at goat tending. He did morning and
evening milking chores and fed the goats. Life
settled into a comfortable routine for him on
the ranch, and he could often be seen in his
baseball cap and blue jeans out in the fields,
working on the fences or tending the goats.
He didn't particularly like the back bedroom
or the water bed in it. He said it was too cold
there. So Williams let him move a sleeping bag
and his clothes into a bathroom and that became Gonzales's room.

It was in July 1991, that Robert Gonzales and
Barbara Muszalski first met. She had come by
to talk with Dave Williams about goat ranching.
Her first impression of Gonzales was that he
was quiet, polite and very sweet. He brought
out all her maternal instincts. He seemed like
such a waif in the modern world. As for Robert
Gonzales, he was smitten by Barbara almost in-
stantly. She was so kind and cheerful. Nobody
had treated him so warmly and with such respect for a long time.

Everything would have been a pastoral idyll
on the Williams ranch except for one thing—

there was another woman living and working there named Patty Millard. There was nothing particularly wrong with Millard, other than she was outspoken. She and Gonzales did not get along from the word go. She sensed there was something wrong with him behind those polite manners and shy ways. Unlike Dave Williams and Barbara Muszalski, she found Gonzales to be "bizarre." And unlike them, she saw him up close every day, while those two were off on other business. Gonzales often would stop his work just to stare at the wind turbine "windmills" up on Altamont Pass behind the Williams ranch. There were six thousand of these spread among the hills, the largest concentration of wind turbines in the world. Generating an immense amount of kilowatts per year, their fifty-eight-foot blades spun round and round in a ceaseless motion as cool breezes from the coast met the warm winds of the inland valleys.

Granted they were fascinating, but Robert Gonzales stared at them with something beyond fascination. It was more like some kind of mania. Even more than this, Millard found him to be "bizarre" when he would pick up a pebble and stare at it in his hand as if it could tell him the future. One day while out in back, she saw him petting a baby goat. Thinking it was an awfully cute scene, she ran to grab her camera and snapped a photo. As soon as he spied her with the camera, he threw the goat to the ground, hopped a fence and ran into the milking barn to hide. When she confronted him about this later, he said, "I don't like having my picture taken."

Things between Robert Gonzales and Patty Millard became increasingly strained in August of 1991. She thought he was incredibly strange and "crazy," while he told her, "You're an evil woman. You're making me sick."

Gonzales did become sick in mid-August—very sick. He was running a high fever and had trouble breathing. Dave Williams took him to Valley Memorial Hospital in Livermore. Gonzales didn't have medical insurance, so he was transferred to Highland Hospital in Oakland that handled uninsured cases. He was diagnosed with tuberculosis and spent the next nine days in the hospital. Since he had tuberculosis, the doctor ran a test to see if he was HIV positive. When the test came back positive, another individual became a very important person in Robert Gonzales's life—AIDS counselor Ivan Meyer.

Their meeting almost didn't happen. For some reason, Gonzales gave the hospital administration a false address in Oakland. When he checked out of the hospital, the letter informing him that he was HIV positive was sent to a nonexistent address in Oakland and was returned stamped "Lost for Follow Up." In late August, Ivan Meyer was leaving the hospital for lunch when he just happened to bump into Robert Gonzales in the corridor. Gonzales had come for a pulmonary test. Meyer then told him that he was HIV positive and that he ought to come and see him for counseling.

Meyer was trained in the field and could help him with financial matters and anything else he wanted to talk about. Gonzales agreed he would come.

True to his word, Gonzales began a regular therapeutic routine with Ivan Meyer, checking his weight and T-cell count. Dave Williams often dropped Gonzales off at Highland Hospital on his way to work in San Francisco. After a while this became too much of a burden as Williams would often show up for work late at the flower shop because of the extra mileage. Good-hearted Barbara Muszalski volunteered to take Gonzales there instead. She was not only a generous person, but she felt sorry for him as well. He seemed like such an innocent at times. In return, his feelings for her became downright infatuation.

As Robert Gonzales struggled with his illness through September and October 1991, his relationship with Patty Millard deteriorated even further. She now thought he was absolutely crazy, while he was more certain than ever that her presence was contributing to his illness. On October 5, 1991, it all came to a head. He and Millard not only got into a shouting match, they got into a shoving match. It got so out of hand that Patty Millard called the Alameda Sheriff's Department to come and quell the disturbance. When Alameda County Sheriff's Deputy Richardson arrived, he pulled the combatants apart and took their statements. He also found out something very strange. The name on Robert Gonzales's

driver's license was Arthur Cruze. Asked about
this, he said he had used that name in southern California.

At a loss how to remedy the situation, Dave
Williams called the Muszalskis and asked if
Gonzales could stay in a fifty-foot mobile home
on their property until things blew over. The
Muszalskis agreed and Gonzales was ecstatic. It
put him even closer to the woman he so ad-
mired.

Even though he was often sick and still going
to therapy at Highland Hospital, October 1991
was one of the happiest months in Gonzales's
life. He followed Barbara Muszalski around the
ranch like a puppy, milked the goats and did
other odd jobs. He wouldn't even allow her to
pay him for his work. Instead, he accepted
homemade chocolates from her that he loved.

Barbara Muszalski was amused by the situation. She could plainly see that Gonzales was
enamored with her. But it was like some teen-
age boy's crush on an older woman. It seemed
so innocent and kind of sweet.

Robert Gonzales was saddened in November
when Dave Williams evicted Patty Millard from
the ranch. It meant he had to go back and live
there. But at least he still looked forward to
the days that Barbara drove him to Highland
Hospital. Just sitting next to her in her Chevy
pickup made him feel a warm glow. He often
phoned her and asked if he could come over
and do odd jobs on her ranch. He wouldn't

ask for any money, just the chocolates she made. Even Jim Muszalski said of the situation, "He was in need, and we were in a position to help." The Muszalskis were those kinds of people. They would help a stray kitten or a stray ranch hand.

But as 1991 turned to 1992, Robert Gonzales was changing. The soft-spoken and friendly young man was turning into a brooding and dour individual. Dave Williams said, "He spent all day in front of the television set, staring off into space. He became very secretive, very quiet, very withdrawn."

Jim Muszalski noticed the changes too. He said, "Robert would spend hours collecting pebbles and staring off at the Altamont Hills. He carried himself in a way that he was always afraid."

God only knows what Robert Gonzales saw when he stared at the windmills whirling on the barren hills of Altamont, but whatever it was he spied there, he could no longer control his own inner demons. He had to tell someone. He decided that the "someone" had to be his AIDS counselor, Ivan Meyer.

In early March 1992, Gonzales revealed to Meyer that he was obsessed with a local woman. In Meyer's own words: "He was very tenacious on the subject. He wouldn't let it go."

Gonzales also said, "If you really knew me, you wouldn't like me. I was a muscleman for the Mafia in Reno and Las Vegas. I've been involved in stabbings and killings."

He didn't give exact locations or dates, but said that he had killed a man in Las Vegas because the man owed him money.

Meyer put all of this down to bragging and some misplaced need to appear macho. But even then, it was the first clue that Robert Gonzales might in fact be something other than he seemed.

If Meyer had any illusions about the obsessive nature of Gonzales's relationship with the mystery woman, these illusions were definitely dispelled on March 9, 1992. Meyer had just invited family members over to his home in Oakland when Gonzales phoned. Gonzales was frantic. He rambled on and on about a woman he couldn't stop thinking of. Meyer asked if he was in love with this woman. Gonzales answered, "Yes." Then he revealed that her name was Barbara. Meyer asked if he had had sex with her. Gonzales said he thought about it all the time, but that he wouldn't do that to her since he was HIV positive. Then he added that she had a husband, but that she didn't really love her husband. Not the way she loved him.

"Can I come over?" Gonzales pleaded. "I've got to talk to you!"

"Not now," Meyer replied. "I've got family visiting."

Gonzales hung up in frustration.

By now not even Barbara Muszalski was amused by the situation with Robert Gonzales. He was phoning her a dozen times a day on the flimsiest excuses just to talk to her. He would take a sackful of quarters to the pay phone at the Lawrence Livermore Lab visitor center and spend half the day calling her. Dave Williams began paying Gonzales his twenty dollars in quarters, on Gonzales's insistence.

Gonzales told Barbara Muszalski on the phone that she no longer loved her husband, Jim. "You and Jim have arguments," he said. "You're not happy."

She countered, "Married people have arguments all the time. I love Jim."

Gonzales began to insinuate that Jim was having an affair behind Barbara's back—which was patently untrue. He said, "He's not Mr. Pure like you think. He's not Mr. Clean."

One day in March 1992, Bill Jones, an itinerant goat breeder, who was now staying in the fifty-foot mobile home on the Muszalski ranch, heard the phone ringing in the main house every fifteen minutes for three hours. Barbara Muszalski would not answer it. When he asked why, she answered, "Because it's Robert calling. It's totally out of control."

Jones tried to make a joke of the situation. "Maybe he's a hit man," he said.

Barbara Muszalski looked him straight in the eye and answered, "Yes." Then she related to Jones that Gonzales had once told her he had done some crimes down in southern California. She thought it was all bluff at the time. Something to make him look more manly in her eyes. Now she didn't know what to believe.

By April, the phone calls did not abate; they became more pervasive and persistent. Very early in the month, Tish Havens, a friend of

Barbara's, was at the Muszalski residence when the phone rang. She picked up the receiver and heard a man's voice on the other end of the line speaking in sensual tones. When she demanded, "Who is this?" he replied, "You know who."

"No, I don't!" she responded angrily, and gave her own name.

Suddenly his voice changed completely to a more businesslike manner. He apologized and said that his name was Robert Gonzales.

By the second week of April, it was all becoming too much for Barbara Muszalski. She was afraid to pick up the phone and let all her calls go on the recorder instead. When her housekeeper, Susan Still, was to be married in mid-April, Barbara Muszalski invited Dave Williams over on April 8 to help with the planning. The ceremony was to be held at the Muszalski ranch house and Williams could help out with the flower arrangements. But when he came over, all she could talk about was the Robert Gonzales situation.

"Robert is totally out of control," she said. "I think he's coming on to me. He told me he fantasized about me in bed. I told him that's ridiculous. I'm old enough to be your mother. But he keeps running Jim down. He insists Jim's having an affair. I finally told him to leave me alone!"

Williams agreed that the situation was intolerable. He began toying with the notion of evicting Gonzales. But before he did, Robert Gonzales got through to Barbara Muszalski one more time by phone on the evening of April 8, 1992. "I need a ride to Highland Hospital tomorrow," he demanded. "So what are you going to do about it?"

"I don't like your tone," she countered.

This made him furious. He began cussing her out.

Outraged, she slammed the phone down on the hook.

A few minutes later, he called back, all apologies. Gonzales was contrite and meek.

"After all I've done for you, I didn't deserve that!" Barbara Muszalski said.

"I know," he answered. "I'm sorry." Then he went on about how sick he really was and how it clouded his judgment.

Good-hearted woman that she was, Barbara Muszalski agreed to drive him to Highland Hospital the next morning.

On Thursday, April 9, 1992, Jim Muszalski left for work on his motorcycle as he always did at seven-thirty in the morning. As he peered over the handlebars, he saw Barbara getting ready to milk the goats. At ten A.M., Barbara's friend Deborah Moyer and her children arrived at the Muszalski house to pick up some baby goats. Moyer was taking them to a local nursery-school class to show to the kids. Barbara Muszalski angrily told her about the previous night's altercation with Robert Gonzales. But then her mood lightened and she talked about Susan Still's upcoming wedding at the ranch on Saturday. She described the preparations she was making.

Deborah Moyer and her children only stayed for fifteen minutes and then had to leave. She said she would be back around two P.M. with the baby goats.

Barbara Muszalski was just about to leave on her way to pick up Gonzales on the Williams ranch, when the phone rang. It was Patty Millard, who now worked and lived in San Francisco. Millard was calling on her break and wanted to talk about old times and goat raising. But Barbara Muszalski was in a hurry and they didn't talk long. To Patty's ear, Barbara seemed unusually subdued. Millard noted in her phone journal that the call ended at 10:59 A.M.

Barbara Muszalski drove her white Chevy S-10 pickup the few miles to the Williams ranch and arrived between 11:05 and 11:10 A.M. Gonzales was already waiting in the yard. If she hoped that he had learned his lesson the night before when he phoned and she had chewed him out, she was sadly disappointed. As soon as he climbed into the cab, he began his obsessive behavior again. He told her once more that Jim wasn't the man for her. Only he was. He insisted that she come with him either to New York or Los Angeles. She told him to stop.

The next few moments became such a blur of unleashed fury that not even Robert Gonzales would remember them in the exact order later on. All he knew was that once again he was being rejected by the woman he loved. He pulled a ten-inch kitchen butcher knife that he had stolen from Dave Williams's kitchen out of his jacket and slashed at her. He felt the knife blade stab into her flesh. Barbara Muszalski threw up her arm to deflect the next blow. But it was all in vain. He cut into her arms, then into her hands. He slashed so viciously that it cut through tendons right down to the bone. He moved on to her upper body, stabbing her in the breasts and abdomen eight times—five of them deep enough to penetrate to the ribs, diaphragm, liver and even the small bowel mesentery. He was in such a frenzy that he slashed at her face three times, in and around her left eye. His final blow into her chest was so savage that it sliced through her aorta and broke off a piece of the knife handle.

By the time his rage was finally spent, he'd stabbed her a total of twenty-two times, leaving her absolutely slaughtered and the inside of the pickup's cab and himself sprayed with blood and gore. There was almost no inch of the interior that wasn't splattered with blood.

Panting and out of breath from his crazed butchery, Gonzales was suddenly aware that there was a vehicle just across the road and the person inside was doing something. He sat quietly while the stranger went about her business and then left up Lupin Way. Only when the vehicle was gone did he drive the blood-spattered pickup, which looked more like a slaughterhouse, up the driveway and behind the barn. Realizing he couldn't just leave Barbara Muszalski in the truck, he dragged her

body out of the cab and stuffed it into the
back of the pickup under the camper shell.
Blood spilled onto the tailgate and license
plate that read JBARSKI Then he pulled apart
some sections of baled hay, called flakes, and
covered the body with them. He grabbed a
couple of blankets that were used by Williams
to wrap up baby goats, and tried to clean the
cab. But it was almost an impossible task. The
blood was everywhere. About the best he could
do was smear it around. Finally he returned to
the house, changed his bloodstained clothes
and packed a few belongings in a couple of
overnight bags. One thing he knew for sure—
neither he nor Barbara Muszalski nor the
pickup could stay there. People were always
dropping by the ranch on business, even when
Williams wasn't there.

About one P.M., a woman goat breeder dropped
by the Muszalski ranch at the time Barbara had
specified to meet her there. Finding no one
home, the woman left after pinning a note to the
gate—"I stopped by and looked at the goat. I
don't think I'm interested in buying it."

A little after two P.M., Deborah Moyer returned to the Muszalski residence with the
baby goats she had taken to the nursery
school. Finding no one at home, she knew
from experience that the Muszalskis never
locked their doors. She let herself in, left a
note and returned the baby goats to their pen.
Then she departed, thinking that Barbara was

out somewhere on business. She didn't think twice about Robert Gonzales.

But Gonzales wasn't quite out of the area yet. At three P.M., Ivan Meyer looked up from his desk at Highland Hospital and was surprised to see Gonzales standing in front of him. He looked awfully agitated and concerned.

"I want to talk to you!" Gonzales insisted.

Meyer answered, "I can't right now. I have two other patients I've got to see. Then it will be five o'clock and time for me to go home."

It looked as if Gonzales wanted to say something more, but decided not to. In disgust, he turned around and went out the door. The main impression he left with counselor Ivan Meyer was, "He looked very needy."

Jim Muszalski returned to his ranch a little after four-thirty P.M. from his job in Silicon Valley. When he first arrived, he noticed that the mail and newspaper had already been picked up, so he motored up the hill on his bike to the house. He was mildly surprised that Barbara wasn't home, knowing that she wanted to work on Susan Still's upcoming wedding. But he wasn't overly concerned—Barbara was always being distracted by something that needed to be picked up for the ranch or the animals.

At five-thirty, Jim was puttering around the house when the phone rang and he fully expected it to be Barbara with an explanation as to why she was late. But it was Robert Gonzales instead. Gonzales asked a very strange question. "Do you know what the phone number is at Dave's ranch?"

Jim Muszalski laughed and said, "You don't know your own phone number?"

"No. I don't call myself!" he snapped. Then he added, "Can you hurry up?"

"All right," Muszalski answered, knowing that Gonzales was awfully strange these days. He gave him the phone number and as soon as he did, Gonzales hung up.

A short time later, Dave Williams came by the Muszalski ranch and was surprised when Barbara wasn't there. They had agreed to meet in the evening so that they could go over the flower arrangements for the wedding. This was unusual. Barbara was a very punctual and considerate person. But there were other things to do, since Jim Muszalski didn't know much about milking the goats. So Williams agreed to milk them while Muszalski did other odd jobs in the yard. By seven-thirty P.M., Williams was still at his task and it began to get dark. Worried now that Barbara might have fallen down somewhere on the ranch and couldn't call for help, Jim went out and walked the entire fence line. But he didn't find her anywhere.

As the sun set across the vineyards of the Livermore Valley on April 9, 1992, Jim Muszalski was on the verge of panic. Dave Williams said he would like to stay and keep him company, but that he had to milk and feed his own animals. Muszalski had lived long enough on a ranch to understand. They were long-time friends and he knew that Dave would stay if he could.

When Williams got home, he called Gonzales's name, but got no answer. He assumed that he was probably still at Highland Hospital. After a quick bite to eat, Williams went out into the pens and began to milk his goats. Then shortly before nine P.M., he received a phone call from Gonzales. In a strange agitated voice, Gonzales asked, "Can you pick me up in town [Livermore]? I've missed the connection from the hospital and the BART [Bay Area Rapid Transit] bus quits running at the lab about seven o'clock."

"Okay," Williams answered. Then as an afterthought, he said, "By the way, did you talk to Barbara today?"

Gonzales immediately became defensive. "No. Why?"

"Well, she's missing and Jim doesn't know where she's at."

Extremely upset now, Gonzales answered, "Well, why are you hassling me about this!"

Surprised by his overreaction, Dave Williams said, "I'm just trying to find out where she's at. We're worried about her."

Evading the issue of Barbara Muszalski, Gonzales insisted, "Are you going to pick me up or not?"

Resigned to Gonzales's strange behavior, Williams sighed and said, "Okay, call me when you get there. I'll pick you up."

"Well, we can talk about Barbara then," Gonzales said.

But Robert Gonzales never did phone Dave Williams again or show up at the bus stop in Livermore. He and the body of Barbara Muszalski and her Chevy pickup simply disappeared. In fact, he wasn't Robert Gonzales at all. Nor was he James Angel, Nick D'Amico or Antonio Perillo. He was an individual who changed names like a chameleon changes its colors. His real name was Benjamin Pedro Gonzales and on the night of April 9, 1992, he seemed to vanish into thin air.

II

AMERICA'S MOST WANTED

Four

The Tag Team

As it grew darker on the evening of April 9, 1992, Jim Muszalski became increasingly worried about his missing wife. Finally around 9:15 P.M., he couldn't stand the suspense any longer. He phoned the Livermore Police Department to make a missing person's report. The officer on duty told him that since he lived outside the city limits, he should call the Alameda Sheriff's Department instead. They would handle everything for him.

At exactly 9:20 P.M. at the Alameda County Sheriff's Office, Officer Morgado was sitting at his desk when the phone rang. He picked up the receiver and heard the voice of a concerned man on the other end of the line who identified himself as James Muszalski. The tape recorder was running and Officer Morgado wrote later in his report, "James told me he last saw his wife at 0830 hours on 4/9/92 as he left for work. Barbara, according to James, was probably dressed in blue sweats, and a T-shirt, clothing she usually wears to do farming chores in. James believes that Barbara was at home until approximately 10:30–11:00 hours due to the farm chores being completed and the mail, which usually arrives about 10:30 hours, gone from the box. It is usually Barbara's habit to collect the mail from the box after completing work and heading to town. James told me she had an appointment at home to sell a goat at 1330 hours, but did not return home.

"James told me he and Barbara have been married 31 years and have had no marital problems. He cited neither mental or medical problems. Barbara is a dependable, reliable person who calls when she is going to be late and leaves messages when necessary. James could offer no explanation for Barbara leaving on her own.

"James did say that Barbara was meeting minor difficulties with a Hispanic male adult who sometimes does work around the house. Apparently, Robert, the Hispanic male adult, has developed an affection for Barbara, and that Barbara has received disturbing phone calls from Robert. James had only limited information about Robert. James told me Robert lived on Lupin Way in Livermore on the northside of the street heading eastbound."

After the phone call was finished, Officer Morgado gave it a designation. It became Alameda County Sheriff's Department case # 92–5408.

A sheriff's department squad car was sent out to the Muszalski ranch and the deputy talked further with Jim. Believing that Barbara might have gone to Dave Williams's ranch, because she had plans to talk with Williams about an upcoming wedding, the officer also drove by that location. But he did not see her Chevy S-10 pickup there, and continued on, slowly driving on the nearby roads, looking for Barbara's vehicle. A likely location was the maze of roads through the Lawrence Livermore Laboratory, but even this search proved unfruitful. It was a long restless night for Jim Muszalski, waiting for word about Barbara, which did not come.

On the following morning, April 10, three men in the Alameda County Sheriff's Department were assigned to the case, and would become an integral part of the Muszalskis' lives for years to come. They were Detective Monte de Coste, Sergeant Dale Toussaint and Sergeant Brian Lerche.

Sergeant Dale Toussaint was well built with brown hair and a thick brown mustache. There was a no-nonsense look about him. Just the way he carried himself would give a "perp" second thoughts about causing any trouble in his presence. Some guys seemed born to wear the khaki color of the sheriff's deputy uniform, and he was one of them. But he was also compassionate and eager to lend a hand to any victim. He instinctively knew the difference between the "good guys" and the "bad guys." The good guys were the victims and they often just needed a sympathetic ear.

Sergeant Toussaint had just recently come

off a case in Alameda County's rural area east
of Livermore that was strikingly similar to the
Dondi Johnson murder in southern California.
Fourteen-year-old Jessica Ann McHenry was
found by the side of a narrow country road.
She had been murdered elsewhere, dropped
there, and then her body set on fire. What was
left of her was not a pretty sight. Sergeant
Toussaint had been frustrated by that case and
he told a *San Jose Mercury News* reporter,
"There was a very small amount of evidence
at the scene. There were no gas cans lying
around."

Obviously he hoped for more clues and better results in what looked to be a missing person's case on the Muszalski ranch.

Sergeant Toussaint was the first law enforcement agent to become involved with Jim
Muszalski. He arrived at the Muszalski ranch
on Tesla Road on the morning of April 10 to
find an increasingly agitated and worried husband with a missing wife. While Jim's children
manned the phones, Muszalski and Sergeant
Toussaint walked through the outbuildings and
fields. No longer believing that Barbara was
just a missing person, Jim now believed that
she was a victim "of foul play" as he put it.
He at least kept the hope alive that she had
just been kidnapped. He didn't want to entertain any worse possibilities. When asked by Sergeant Toussaint who might be involved, Jim
Muszalski immediately answered, "Robert Gonzales!"

Muszalski showed Sergeant Toussaint a note

Barbara had scribbled on a note pad just a few days before. In dark bold letters was written: "Robert—chocolates." Obviously it meant she was to deliver him some more of the homemade chocolates he loved.

Sergeant Toussaint could plainly see that Jim Muszalski was very upset and worried about his wife. He jotted down in his notebook, "Jim's emotions are close to the surface."

Sergeant Toussaint then spoke with handyman Bill Jones, who was living in the mobile home out back. Jones related the crank phone calls that Barbara had been receiving from Gonzales, and his constant attentions to her. When Jones spoke of his joke about Robert probably hiding out and being a hit man, and Barbara's reply, "Yes"—Sergeant Toussaint's ears perked up and he jotted the conversation down in his notebook.

Barbara Muszalski's daughter, Jamie, added that her mother often gave Gonzales rides to Highland Hospital. "That's just the kind of person she is," she stated. "He kept coming on to her, but he never touched her. She was more motherly toward him."

There was at least enough evidence on hand now to suspect that Robert Gonzales might have something to do with Barbara Muszalski's disappearance.

Later that day, another key officer from the Alameda County Sheriff's Department joined Sergeant Toussaint on the Muszalski case. He was Sergeant Brian Lerche. Friendly and outgoing, Sergeant Lerche was nonetheless a thorough and dedicated cop. He had served in the Lake County, Illinois, Sheriff's Office from 1968 to 1973 before moving to California. Once he joined the homicide unit of the Alameda County Sheriff's Department, he never looked back. He was one of those guys made for the job. He had a good eye for detail and the persistence that were prerequisites for the field. By 1992, he'd already been involved in nearly one hundred murder cases and had helped solve many of them.

A bulletin about the missing woman and a description of her Chevy pickup was distributed to local newspapers, radio stations and television stations throughout the Bay Area by the Alameda County Sheriff's Department. The reports noted the unusual license plate on the vehicle—JBARSKI. The pickup also had a bumper sticker on the back that stated GOAT MILK MAKES YOU HORNY. In response, calls started flooding in about the woman and truck from all over the area—some of them wildly off the mark. But the police couldn't discount anything just yet.

Donna Adams called in and said that she and her husband were driving on I-580 west of Livermore on the Dublin Grade in the early afternoon on April 9 when she spotted a white pickup bearing the license plate JBARSKI. She remembered trying to figure out what the license plate meant.

Another tipster thought he had seen the same pickup in Pleasanton, ten miles away, with a man and woman inside. They were also headed westbound.

There were numerous calls about a white pickup traveling on I-580 eastbound, westbound, inbound, outbound—nothing could be discarded at this point. Both Sergeant Toussaint and Sergeant Lerche knew that every crime had a lot of chaff that went along with the wheat. It was all part of the process and nothing could be discarded in the initial stages.

At Malley's Restaurant in Livermore, a waitress remembered a young Hispanic man who matched the description of Robert Gonzales coming in on April 9 and asking for a pay phone. He told her he worked at the N3 Cattle Company. He made his call, ordered a chicken sandwich and then left.

Ralph Seichter, who had been standing at the Mesquite Gate of the Lawrence Livermore Laboratory on the morning of April 9, spotted a white Chevy pickup with a camper shell on the back slowly driving up Vasco Road toward I-580 about eleven-thirty A.M. He distinctly remembered the Chevy logo on the tailgate.

While Sergeants Toussaint and Lerche gathered in the phone calls, Deputy Francis Silva was dispatched to Dave Williams's ranch on April 10 with a search and rescue team. This was still a missing person's case and there was a chance that Barbara Muszalski was incapacitated and lying somewhere on the ranch, either in tall grass or one of the outbuildings. While the search and rescue team spread out over the property, Deputy Silva stayed closer to the house and driveway. By mid-morning, he found something very interesting and wrote it down in his notebook.

"There is a driveway behind the house between the backyard of the house and the first chicken house on the left. In this driveway were two patches of dirt with a dark red stain, which appeared to be blood. These two stains were collected. . . . On the door jamb (of the kitchen door) were stains of what appeared to be dried blood. On the cabinet doors just below the kitchen sink were more stains of what appeared to be dried blood. On the splash wall on the left side of the kitchen faucets was another stain which appeared to be dried blood. I took photographs of the stains and collected the stains from these locations. The samples were air dried prior to placing them into evidence. On the bathroom vanity was a glass with a toothbrush inside. I checked for latent prints on this glass. I received two latent prints from the glass in the living room and received one latent lift. In the bedroom were six empty cans of Coca Cola. I checked for latent prints on these cans and recovered one latent lift. All four latent prints were marked. Hay from the barn was collected."

Latent prints are made when natural oils and perspiration present between the fingertip ridges are transferred to a surface by touch. Hard surfaces are usually dusted with fingerprint powder, which sticks to the traces of oil and perspiration left by the fingertip. Powders come in different colors and the investigator chooses the one that provides the most contrast with the object being dusted. Fine carbon powder is used on light-colored surfaces, while aluminum powder reveals prints on dark surfaces. A fiberglas latent-print brush is used to dust the surfaces and then a latent-print lifting tape is applied.

Even clothing and non-slick surfaces such as paper can be examined for prints. An iodine fuming method is used. The item is placed in an enclosed cabinet with iodine crystals and then heated. The iodine vapor given off by the crystals combines with the traces of the print and leaves a visible pattern. Another method is ninhydrin spray that forms a purple-blue color when combined with traces of amino acids from human perspiration left by touch.

Meanwhile, Alameda County Sheriff's Sergeant Roderick was doing a similar search at the Muszalski ranch and home. He examined not only the house, but the outbuildings and extensive grounds. The entire operation lasted from early morning until three P.M.

On the following day, April 11, Sergeant Toussaint was still trying to figure out exactly who Robert Gonzales was. Everyone who knew him had only sketchy details about his past or even his name. Most only knew him as "Robert." The incident with Patty Millard from the previous fall brought up the driver's license he had produced that said he was Arthur Cruze from southern California.

Obviously this guy moved around a lot, and

seemed to change his name as well. He had
mentioned to people on the Muszalski and
Williams ranches that he had been in Los Angeles, Las Vegas, Dallas, Chicago and New York.
Sergeant Toussaint phoned Valley Memorial
Hospital in Livermore for Robert Gonzales's
medical records, and did the same at Highland
Hospital in Oakland. Then he called the California Department of Motor Vehicles and
learned Robert Gonzales had once registered
as Robert G. Gonzales in Costa Mesa, California, just below Los Angeles. He had given a
street address on Ramona Drive.

Sergeant Toussaint contacted Officer Walterscheid in southern California and asked him
to go to that address. When Walterscheid arrived, he spoke with a Hispanic man who identified himself as Rudolfo Martinez. What the
man said next took everyone by surprise and
gave Jim Muszalski new hope that Barbara was
still alive. Martinez said, "A woman driving a
white Chevy pickup truck came to my house.
I told her to go away."

Sergeants Toussaint and Lerche were immediately on a plane bound for southern California, following up on this new lead. It seemed
odd that Barbara Muszalski would suddenly
show up in Costa Mesa, just to be turned away
by a Hispanic man at Gonzales's old address.
But who knew what the circumstances were?
She might be in shock and acting strangely after some terrible ordeal.

Things became even more intriguing when
Sergeants Toussaint and Lerche showed Offi-

cer Walterscheid a sketchy photo of Robert
Gonzales of Livermore. "Yes," Walterscheid
said, "that's the person I talked to."

Sergeants Toussaint and Lerche immediately
went to the address on Ramona Drive in Costa
Mesa, but Rudolfo Martinez wasn't at home.
However, they did talk to Manuel Burguez and
showed him the photo. Their initial hope
turned to disappointment. Burguez said, "That
picture looks like my brother, but it's not him.
And I don't know any Robert Gonzales."

Disappointed, but not yet through with
southern California or the fact that Barbara
Muszalski might still be alive and being held
against her will, Sergeants Toussaint and Lerche visited the Rampart Division of the Los Angeles Police Department on April 12. From
them they learned that Gonzales had possibly
once lived in an apartment on Ninth Street in
Los Angeles. But when they checked it out, the
manager said he didn't know him or have any
recollection of the man living there.

Sergeants Toussaint and Lerche were still op-
timistic on April 12, but events in northern
California were just about to overtake them.

At four-thirty P.M. on April 12, June Luzarraga and her husband parked their car on
Level 5, Section A of the short-term parking
garage at San Francisco International Airport.
They were there to pick up relatives arriving
on an American Airlines flight. It took almost
an hour to meet their relatives, collect their

baggage and make their way back to the parking lot. About five-thirty P.M., all of them headed toward the Luzarraga car, the relatives chatting with the husband, when June suddenly spotted a white pickup with the sticker—GOAT MILK MAKES YOU HORNY—on the back. The pickup was parked only two spaces away from her car.

June Luzarraga had seen an article that very morning in the San Ramon newspaper describing the missing Livermore woman and her pickup truck. The article had mentioned the unusual bumper sticker.

She couldn't see into the tinted windows of the camper shell, so she wrote down the license plate, JBARSKI, on a scrap of paper, and noted the space it was parked in—Number 13. She also wrote down the words of another bumper sticker on the pickup. It read LIVERMORE SHOP AND WIN. She couldn't remember all the details of the newspaper article she'd read, so she decided she would recheck it when she got home.

At around eight-thirty P.M., the Luzarragas arrived at their home and June picked up the San Ramon newspaper and reread the article. All the information she'd noted about the pickup at San Francisco International Airport was the same. She immediately called the Alameda County Sheriff's Department.

Sergeant Brian Lerche had just settled in from his disappointing southern California sojourn when the phone rang. Whatever tiredness and lethargy he was feeling was soon dispelled by June Luzarraga's phone call. This was the most concrete evidence he and Sergeant Toussaint had received in three days.

Sergeant Lerche called the Security Office at San Francisco International Airport and contacted Officer K. Moss. "Go up to Level 5 and check out a white Chevy pickup in Space 13," he said. "Then let me know if it's there."

Officer Moss did as instructed and called Lerche back within five minutes. "Yes," he said. "It's the truck with the license plate JBARSKI."

"Okay," Sergeant Lerche said, "hold it as a crime scene until I get there."

After a long day of flying and driving around the roads of southern California, Sergeants Lerche and Toussaint were ready to make one more journey. If they had any doubts as to whether Barbara Muszalski was still alive, they kept them to themselves. Alameda Sheriff's Deputy W. Gordillo was also along for the ride to do tech duties. They all arrived at the Ampco Parking Lot, Level 5, Section A, Space 13 late in the evening.

Making a complete walking inspection around the pickup, they noticed that the tires had been marked several times by the parking lot attendant with chalk, denoting how many days it had been there. From the chalk marks they could tell the pickup had been parked there for at least three days. As they walked around, they also noted a reddish-brown stain on the Chevy's tailgate. Deputy Gordillo took out his 35-mm camera and snapped twenty-four exposures of the tailgate area. Sergeant

Brian Lerche and Gordillo dusted the exterior of the pickup for fingerprints. They also noticed dark reddish-brown sprinkles on the driver's side door handle consistent with dried blood. Looking through the driver's side window, Sergeant Lerche noticed a *Tri-Valley Herald* newspaper dated April 9, 1992, on the dashboard. There were also two blankets covering the seats. One was brown and one was blue.

Sergeant Toussaint, who was in charge of the operation, now ordered technician Gordillo to open the tailgate. As soon as he did, Officer Gordillo noted, "Two flat, yellowish, soiled tennis shoes, pointing with toes up, underneath hay wafers." There was a sudden stench of a strong odor consistent with that of a dead body emanating from the camper shell.

"Okay," Sergeant Toussaint said, "let's freeze the scene and get the crime lab guys out here."

Then all three of them waited in silence with whoever was dead under the hay. None of them had doubts as to who they would find there.

By the time the Alameda County Crime Lab technicians arrived, it was one A.M. on a new day, April 13, 1992. The Alameda County coroner also arrived at about the same time.

The Crime Lab technicians were an experienced bunch, headed up by criminalist Sharon Binkley-Smith. All of them had been on previous high-profile murder cases and they were proficient at their craft. They had seen this type of scene many times before.

The interior of the cab immediately told a tale of incredible violence. Whoever had done it had tried to wipe up the blood with the blankets, but all they had succeeded in doing was soaking up some blood and smearing the rest around. There was blood everywhere. Almost every square inch of the cab had bloodstains on it. The amount of blood was so extensive that it was decided to do the examination at a more secure location under strict guidelines and procedures.

Finally, it was time to see who wore the tennis shoes that protruded from beneath the hay. Sergeant Toussaint ordered the hay removed and Sergeant Lerche and Officer Gordillo slowly began removing the hay wafers, exposing legs, light pink pants and the decomposing body of a white female adult. One look at her face left them in no doubt as to her identity. It was the badly mutilated body of Barbara Muszalski.

Sergeant Toussaint requested a vehicle from Arroyo Towing, which often handled police work, and in the early morning hours of April 13, the Chevy S-10 was loaded aboard a car carrier and taken to the Emergency Services garage in Alameda County across the bay.

Paul Herrmann is an expert forensic pathologist and on April 13, 1992, he performed an autopsy on Barbara Muszalski's body. In his report he wrote, "The body was in a rather advanced state of decomposition and there were numerous and incised wounds on her body. The incised wounds involving her face and hands involved the soft tissue only. In some cases the hands involved the tendons as well. The stab wounds of the body—there were eight of them—five of these penetrated deeply into the body involving the ribs, diaphragm, and the liver. One of them involved the aorta and one of them involved the small bowel mesentery. As a result of the stab wounds that penetrated deep in her body, she had a great deal of blood present in her abdomen and a great deal of blood present in her chest. She had fifteen incised wounds, i.e., cutting wounds, in all. Three of these involved her left eye and the others involved her hands and right wrist."

Later in the report, he described in greater detail the nature of the wounds. He wrote:

Wound #1—On the right breast—moderate.

Wound #2—Just below the right breast. It passes through the tissues and enters the chest cavity through the sixth intercostal space of the right side. It passes directly through the diaphragm without striking the lung and enters the liver to the depth of one inch.

Wound #3—A large wound involving the mid-portion of the lower chest and extending down into the abdomen. [It] penetrates through the chest just to the left of the xiphoid. . . . It then penetrates through the diaphragm inferior to the heart and enters the left lobe of the liver. It passes entirely through the left lobe of the liver, exiting on its posterior surface. It continues toward the spine and enters the anterior wall of the aorta at approximately the level of the tenth and eleventh thoracic vertebrae.

Wound #7—To the right of the umbilicus, passes through the skin and subcutaneous tissue and enters the abdominal cavity. It misses the small bowel but causes a stab wound within the small bowel mesentery.

Wound #8—A puncture wound in the right side of the abdomen.

Conclusion—Barbara Muszalski died of shock and hemorrage due to multiple stab wounds.

At this point, both Sergeants Toussaint and Lerche were pretty sure that Robert Gonzales was their killer. After all, he had been bothering Barbara Muszalski constantly by phone and he was suddenly missing. But they weren't really sure who he was. Sergeant Toussaint ordered a search of Valley Memorial Hospital in Livermore, of "[All] its premises, structures, rooms and receptacles," just in case he was hiding there. Then he ordered a similar search for Highland Hospital in Oakland. Even though the entire area was searched, Robert Gonzales was nowhere to be found.

Lieutenant Ted Nelson of the Alameda County Sheriff's Department told a *Valley Times* reporter on April 14, "We think he's gone and no two ways about it. We feel there's a good possibility he has left the state, not to Mexico or another country, but out of the state."

This assumption was based on Barbara Muszalski's pickup being left at San Francisco International Airport and an agent at one of the ticket counters remembering that on April 9 someone who looked like Robert Gonzales inquired about an out-of-state airline ticket.

At this point it was just as difficult for Sergeants Toussaint and Lerche to figure out who "Robert Gonzales" was, as it was to figure out where he had gone. The driver's licenses already revealed that he had called himself Arthur Cruze and Robert G. Gonzales. They visited various Bay Area cities trying to track down his identity. Sergeant Toussaint told a *Valley Times* reporter, "We are trying to find out who he is, so we can figure out where he is."

On the fourteenth, Roy Marzioli, supervisor of the Alameda County Consolidated Criminal Records Section, informed Sergeant Toussaint that fingerprints lifted from Dave Williams's house by Officer Silva positively matched those of a man with a record. His name was Benjamin Pedro Gonzales. He may have called himself by many names, but that was who he actually was. A computer file showed that he sometimes called himself Ben Gonzales, Ron Gonzales, Santiago Ron Gonzales and "Cheeco."

Mary Caruthers of the California Department of Corrections was able to confirm what Roy Marzioli had found. She pulled up a computer file and photo of a man who had served time in a state prison in southern California for an assault with a deadly weapon in 1985. His photo matched that of the Robert Gonzales they sought, but the name was again Benjamin Pedro Gonzales.

Bit by bit, both Sergeants Toussaint and Lerche were getting an idea of whom they were dealing with. The DMV photo and Department of Corrections photos were incredibly important evidence. Now at least they could do a photo lineup with the people who had known the man in Livermore as Robert Gonzales. On the fourteenth, Sergeant Lerche ran a DMV photo lineup using the photograph of a man who had called himself Dino Cruze on his driver's license. Dave Williams looked at the six photos displayed and said, "Number two, that's the closest one to it. The eyes, the eyebrows, and the ears."

Sergeant Lerche: "Do you think the person in number two [position] is Robert Gonzales?"

Dave Williams: "Heavier in the face, but that looks exactly like him."

Before Barbara Muszalski's friend, Tish Havens, came into the room, Sergeant Lerche switched the photos around so that Gonzales's [Cruze's] photo was in the fourth spot.

Tish Havens said, "The closest how I remember him . . . because his hair was longer and pulled back and he had a cap on . . . but I can't get a definite person. But for some reason number four looks most like him. Something about the eyes and face."

Barbara's friend Deborah Moyer was brought in, but she could not make a positive identification.

Finally it was Jim Muszalski's turn. Gonzales's photo was in the number one spot. Jim took one look at the photos and said, "Number one looks close enough to be him."

On April 16, another photo lineup was conducted using the Department of Corrections photo of Benjamin Gonzales. This time it was one photo in twelve. Once again the photo was placed in various locations. Trish Havens picked number five, Dave Williams number three, and Jim Muszalski number six. All of them picked a photo of Benjamin Gonzales.

Trish Havens said, "Something about the face. Number five sticks out at me and says that's him."

Dave Williams said, "Gonzales is a little thinner in the face, but that's the person I know as Gonzales."

Jim Muszalski was the most direct of all. He pointed at number six and said, "That's him!"

Sergeant Lerche and Detective Monte de Coste also had another important interview that day. They were out at Dave Williams's ranch when they spotted rural route mail carrier Katherine Cleek delivering mail to Williams's roadside mailbox at 11:10 that morning. Noting that Barbara Muszalski had disappeared about that time of day on April 9, they asked her if she had seen anything suspicious at the Williams's ranch on that day. Indeed she had. Ms. Cleek arrived in her Jeep between 11:05 and 11:15 A.M. as usual and spotted a white pickup in Williams's driveway. She remembered it because she had never seen any vehicle parked in that manner before. It was only partially pulled into the driveway and about thirty feet from where she delivered the mail across the road. She noticed it had a camper shell on the back.

Katherine Cleek had no way of knowing at the time how lucky she was. In all likelihood Benjamin Gonzales had probably just finished butchering Barbara Muszalski and was sitting with her dead body in the cab when Katherine drove up to deliver the mail. Had she approached the house with a package or certified letter, she too could have easily become a victim.

Once she'd delivered Williams's mail, she continued up Lupin Way and noticed that the strange white pickup was still there when she made her loop and passed the house on the way back, about five minutes later. This was the best clue so far that the detectives had for a time frame on Barbara Muszalski's death. When Katherine Cleek looked at the photo they produced of Muszalski's pickup she said, "Yes, that looks like the one I saw."

Bit by bit the pieces of the puzzle were coming together about who had perpetrated the terrible crime and when he had done it.

Dave Williams was devastated by Barbara's brutal murder and he blamed himself in part for having introduced "Robert" Gonzales to her. Of course, he couldn't have known at the time about Gonzales's tendencies, but he was a sensitive person and felt utterly crushed by the brutal crime that had ripped apart the lives of his friends, the Muszalskis. But devastated or not, he was a key witness in this case, and Alameda Sheriff's deputies were in and out of his house for several days after the twelfth of April. When Sergeant Lerche asked him if anything was missing, Williams discovered that two old blankets were gone from the laundry room. A blue blanket and a brown one that had been used to wrap baby goats in after they were born. He also discovered that a couple of knives were missing from a matched set in the kitchen. He drew a diagram of the missing knives—one had a serrated twelve-inch blade and the other one a ten-inch blade. Along with these was a missing hunting knife that was used for skinning and butchering rabbits. It had a good sturdy blade. Williams shuddered when he thought about how Gonzales might have used this knife for something other than skinning rabbits.

Along with these items, Sergeant Lerche wanted to know where Williams got his hay. It had already been discovered that the hay used to cover Barbara Muszalski's dead body did not come from the Muszalski ranch. Williams showed Sergeant Lerche his hay stacked in the barn and said he always got it from a rancher he knew in Manteca, about thirty miles away. When he looked over his bales of hay, he noticed that several "flakes" of hay were missing. A flake is a piece of the bale about four or five inches wide and as long as the bale is. When the hay in Barbara Muszalski's pickup was compared to the hay in Williams's barn, it was discovered that they matched, and another puzzle piece fell into place.

Definitive proof that Robert Gonzales was in fact Benjamin Pedro Gonzales came when Sergeant Toussaint contacted Linda Eisnach, Section Chief of the Colorado Department of Health. She located a birth certificate that had the correct date of birth and correct name of whom they were looking for—Benjamin Gonzales, not Robert Gonzales. It also gave his father's name, Benjamin Guzman Gonzales and mother's maiden name, Jennie Mary Roybal. Benjamin Pedro Gonzales was born on August 31, 1959—not the fake date he had given on his Arthur Cruze driver's license.

Three Alameda County Sheriff's officers by now were working in a "tag team" approach to this difficult case. While one explored a particular avenue, the others went in different directions. Then they compared information later. Detective Monte de Coste, Sergeant Dale Toussaint and Sergeant Brian Lerche were leaving nothing to chance.

Detective Monte de Coste applied for a phone records search with Pacific Telephone.

He already knew from Dave Williams that Gonzales often called from the pay phone near the Lawrence Livermore Laboratory visitor center. In his application for a phone records search, Detective de Coste wrote, "Your affiant knows that a trap number search and toll records check could lead to the whereabouts of suspect Ben Gonzales. Your affiant prays an order to the above facts for the Pacific Bell Company to turn over any trap number search and toll records information on the following numbers." Then he gave a list of pertinent numbers. A judge approved the request and so ordered that it be done.

This phone number search had almost immediate positive results. It was discovered that Benjamin Gonzales had phoned his mother in San Jose a few days before the murder of Barbara Muszalski from the pay phone outside the lab's visitor center. Sergeant Toussaint interviewed Gonzales's mother, Jenny, by phone and she said she'd been living at her current address in San Jose for eight months. She hadn't seen Ben in person for a year, and that had been when she lived in Sacramento. Prior to that she hadn't seen him in five years. She didn't even know that he had spent some time in prison in southern California until Sergeant Toussaint told her so. She said her son really didn't talk about himself very much, but usually asked about family members. Even though he dropped from view for years at a time and he moved around a lot, he always seemed to be able to find her. He was the oldest of ten siblings and his brothers, Jesse, Christopher and James were scattered in different states, along with approximately seventy cousins nationwide.

Sergeant Toussaint drew in his breath at that. If Ben Gonzales was staying with relatives, there was a lot of ground to cover.

Sergeant Toussaint asked Jenny where Benjamin might go if he were in trouble. She thought about it and said he might show up at his cousin Paul Roybal's house in Fresno. He seemed to like Paul pretty well. Then she dropped a bombshell. Benjamin had called her only a few days ago—after the murder on April 9. She thought it was from a pay phone because she could hear street noises in the background. He said that he had been sick, but that he was all right now. Then he asked about other family members and how she was doing.

At this point Sergeant Toussaint told Jenny Gonzales that he wanted to talk to her son about the brutal murder of Barbara Muszalski. It was Jenny's turn to be stunned. She said he might be capable of petty crimes, but she didn't think he could kill anyone. He was the quiet one in the family. Nonetheless, she agreed to cooperate with police if he showed up at her house.

Meanwhile, Sergeant Brian Lerche contacted Benjamin's sister, Angelina Gonzales. From her he learned that a couple of their brothers were serving time in state prison. She didn't keep in contact with either Ben or any of her other brothers. She was trying to get her own act

together. She hardly even knew Benjamin anymore and hadn't seen him in years. But she
too agreed to cooperate with police if he suddenly did show up.

Detective Monte de Coste was following an
independent trail that also led toward Ben's
cousin Paul Roybal in Fresno. From old DMV
records, he discovered that Benjamin Gonzales
(aka Dino Art Cruze) had given an address on
Mahoney Drive in San Jose. When Detective de
Coste arrived there, no one knew Ben Gonzales, but they did know Paul Roybal and gave
an address in Fresno.

Detective de Coste crossed his fingers that
Benjamin Gonzales was hiding out at the Roybal residence and faxed the Fresno Police a
wanted poster that his office had just printed
up. It portrayed Gonzales's DMV and Department of Corrections photos and read:

Gonzales, Ben DOB 8/31/59
Hispanic Male—5'7"
180 lbs
black hair, small ponytail, brown bushy
moustache

"The Sheriff's Department is interested in
any information or unusual circumstances or
persons noted by lab employees while in the
area of Lupin Way east of Greenville Road.
This incident occurred at ranch [address num-
ber] on Lupin Way which is about one quarter
mile east of the visitor center on Thursday,

04/09/92, between 10:30 A.M. and the early afternoon hours."

Then there was a photo of Barbara Muszalski's truck, front and rear view.

At the bottom of the flyer was a phone number where the person could contact Sergeant Dale Toussaint or Sergeant Brian Lerche.

On the evening of April 17, two Fresno police officers dropped by Paul Roybal's house to talk about his cousin Benjamin Gonzales. Roybal hadn't seen Gonzales in three years, but just like Jenny Gonzales, he had received a phone call from him only three days earlier—after the murder. Even more incredible than that, Ben Gonzales had called only an hour before the police officers arrived. He had mostly talked about what Roybal and his family had been doing. Roybal asked where he was and Gonzales said, "You don't want to know!"

Paul Roybal doubted that Gonzales was still in Alameda County since he had no relatives there. Also, he knew that two of the other Gonzales brothers were in state prison and the other was a truck driver who could be anywhere. Roybal allowed the officers to search his house and property. They came up empty-handed.

As the sun set behind Pleasanton Ridge on April 17, 1992, Detective Monte de Coste, and Sergeants Dale Toussaint and Brian Lerche were busier than ever with the new information on their main suspect. But on the following morning, all their work would come to a halt. Not because they were tired or discouraged—far from it. Their work would stop because they all wanted to attend the memorial service for Barbara Muszalski.

Five

Valley of Fear

There would be a private funeral for Barbara Muszalski with family members only at a later date, but the memorial service on Saturday, April 18, was not about her death. It was about her life. Jim Muszalski told a *Valley Times* reporter, "It will be a chance for people who knew her to get together and talk about the wonderful things she did. There are a lot of memories to be shared."

Jim told a *Tri-Valley Herald* reporter, "She was my best friend. I've been in love with her for thirty-seven years. She raised three great children. And our forties and fifties were going to be our golden years."

Then he dwelled on more pressing and immediate matters—the herd of goats she left behind. "When all this dies down, I'll be out here and alone, and I certainly can't care for the goats myself."

In response to his needs, local ranchers agreed to buy all the goats. They were the kind of people who helped friends in need. Muszalski said, "I have fifteen cooked meals in the freezer, more food than I know what to do with."

At least for now, before he truly was alone, he had his three children to help him—Brett, twenty-seven, Jamie, twenty-four, and Walter, twenty-three.

On Saturday April 18, the throng began to filter into the Muszalski ranch to remember the life of Barbara Muszalski. Before the day was done, more than two hundred people would attend the gathering. It was so large an affair that two-way radios were used to direct parking, and long tables were set up with food and drinks. Friends and family agreed that it was a party Barbara would have enjoyed. It was also agreed upon that at least on this day tears would be left behind. Instead, it would be a day of laughter, hugging and memories.

Handyman Bill Jones looked out over the crowd and told a reporter, "Barbara was the hub of everything. She was always the one you called when you had a problem."

Shirley Volkman of Livermore recalled, "She was always doing for other people. She was generous, energetic and caring."

Maria Palazzolo said, "I met Jim and Barbara Muszalski twenty years ago. I was always welcomed into their home for parties and celebrations and good company. I spent Christmas at their home for many years. The last Christmas I spent with them, Barb asked me to bring over my recipe for homemade crackers that I had made the year before. And I surprised her with not only the recipe but a basketful of difficult-to-make crackers. She was so appreciative that I planned on making them every Christmas for her just to see that wonderful smile. That was the Christmas before Barb was murdered. She never had the chance to make those crackers, and I never again had the chance to see that wonderful smile."

Barbara's mother, Marie Schlick, was also there and told the *Valley Times* reporter, "My daughter and I used to chat every morning. She was so good. Everybody loved her. I don't know what I'm going to do without her."

She also said later, "Barb was a very contented baby and student. Good student and loving person. Never any trouble. Barb met a wonderful man. He became her husband. Was a loving mother to three children. There is a big empty place in my heart without Barbara. Such a wonderful person Barbara was. She did not deserve to die such a horrible death."

Jan Gonzalez, a longtime friend of Barbara's, related, "I miss my friend terribly. Barbara was the most giving person I know. She accepted people at face value. She had an incredible zest for life. We had a running joke between us. How could a big-city, career girl like me have anything in common with the goat lady? I don't think we ever figured it out. It really didn't matter.

"I have such wonderful memories of her. She introduced me to a world full of wonders. But most of all, my husband and I found a

true family who we could belong to after we
moved to the Bay Area.

"The hurt will never go away. I will forever
hear her laugh when I think of her, which is
often. She will forever be in my heart."

Then Jan realized that people often try to
paint the deceased in glowing terms at a memorial service. So she said, "The last thing you
want to do is idealize somebody when they die,
but I idealized her while she was alive."

Beneath all the memories and general good
feelings was a darker subtext—the loss of innocence for the area. Brutal murder had come
to Tesla Road and the killer was still on the
loose. It made people afraid. Lloyd Marsh, a
Tesla Road resident, told the *Valley Times* reporter, "I never locked my door for thirty
years. I do it all the time now. Before, you
could knock on a neighbor's door. Now it
scares them to death if you do it at night. I
warned my wife not to open the door for
strangers. You can't trust anybody, anymore."

Sandy Mantz, another rural area resident,
agreed. "We're considering installing automatic gates. You have to be cautious about who
comes on the property. We've been out here
thirteen years and we're more aware than we
used to be."

There were a lot of transients and drifters
moving through the rural area east of Livermore and that was the rub. They were the only
ones willing to take low-paying, labor-intensive
jobs. Betty Clamp, the owner of a hundred-acre
cattle ranch, told the *Valley Times* reporter,

"You have to rely on someone willing to come in and work for what small amount a rancher can afford."

To contend with this dilemma, Lloyd Marsh said he would keep his eye on several neighbors' places while they were away at work during the daytime. A neighborhood crime watch group was formed.

So along with all the hugging and remembering of Barbara Muszalski, there was also a constant reminder that Benjamin (aka Robert) Gonzales was still at large. The stack of "Wanted for Murder" fliers on a table displaying his mugshot attested to that. A reward fund consisting of corporate funds was organized by Jim Muszalski in hopes someone would come forward with clues to Gonzales's whereabouts.

Sergeant Dale Toussaint and Sergeant Brian Lerche were also there among the crowd, and they told Jim Muszalski of the latest developments in the case. Sergeant Toussaint explained about all the contacts with Ben Gonzales's relatives and he said, "These contacts open more doors we'll have to explore." He also told Muszalski one more thing that was encouraging. A municipal court judge had just issued a no-bail, probable-cause arrest warrant.

"Probable cause" is defined by the Supreme Court as "a reasonable ground for the belief, less than evidence justifying in a conviction, but more than bare suspicion. Probable cause concerns circumstances in which a person of reasonable caution would believe an offense

has been or is being committed." Probable
cause evidence can come from witnesses, evidence found at a crime scene and forensic in-
vestigations. With the issuance of the arrest
warrant it gave the detectives "extremely intru-
sive powers," including a directive to all law
enforcement officers in the state to arrest Benjamin Gonzales.

After all the reminiscing, the fact remained
that Benjamin Gonzales needed to be found
before he could be brought to justice. The battle was being waged on two fronts now—the
direct on-the-street approach by Detective
Monte de Coste, Sergeant Dale Toussaint and
Sergeant Brian Lerche, and the antiseptic, very
controlled approach in the crime lab tech
rooms. Just like the trio of law enforcement
officers, there were three main criminalists in
the Alameda County Sheriff's Office crime labs
dealing with the case—Kurtis Smith, Raquel
Craft and Sharon Binkley-Smith.

Kurtis Smith had been a criminalist with the
Alameda County Sheriff's Department for six
years. He was an expert in fingerprint processing and lifting latent prints, or as he explained
it, "The development of latent prints and the
enhancement of patent prints. A latent print
is when it's invisible. A patent print when it is
visible."

Smith had college training in the art and sci-
ence of fingerprint collection, as well as at the
Oakland Police Department Crime Lab and

California Department of Justice Crime Lab. As far as the Benjamin Gonzales case went, he now had Barbara Muszalski's dismantled tailgate in his lab. In his report, he wrote, "I dusted the tailgate with black chemical powder to enhance the patent area. Then photographed them. Then chemically treated them with amido-black, which is a biological stain which reacts with proteins in blood to stain it a dark purple. Then I photographed it again."

These photographs were sent to criminalist Raquel Craft, who had been with the Alameda County Sheriff's Department crime lab for ten years and was also a fingerprint expert. She processed the evidence and accessed the California I.D. automatic latent print system. She came up with a probable match from the tailgate photos in the Department of Justice files. The right index fingerprint from Barbara Muszalski's Chevy tailgate matched that of a former convict—Benjamin Pedro Gonzales.

Meanwhile, criminalist Sharon Binkley-Smith was hard at work in the lab in another area. She initially delved into the rape kit concerning Barbara Muszalski that had been obtained by the coroner. The vaginal swabs and oral swabs both came up negative for semen, as did Barbara's panties. She had not been raped or forced to orally copulate the suspect. Foreign hairs found on her body, which might have come from the killer and contain DNA samples, were also analyzed.

Hairs were a good source of useful evidence because they retained their structure for a long period of time and did not degrade. The reason for this was their tough outer covering, known as the cuticle. Within the cuticle cortex, a regular array of cells ran down the length of the hair and carried the particles of pigment that gave hair its various colors. The way in which the particles were shaped and distributed and their precise color could help identify specific individuals.

Within the center of the cortex was another inner layer of cells called the medulla. By a process called neutron activation analysis, Binkley-Smith could bombard the hair with neutrons. The neutrons would collide with atoms of the different trace elements making up the sample and render them radioactive. By measuring the gamma radiation, the most minute traces of every constituent could be measured. The likelihood of two individuals having the same concentration of the prime constituents was about one in a million.

But Binkley-Smith didn't have to go that far. By intense magnification alone, she could see that the hairs that came from Barbara Muszalski's body were animal hairs.

Even the supposed blood that Deputy Silva had collected at Dave Williams's ranch from the driveway, kitchen and door jambs proved to be disappointing. The samples were all from animal blood.

Sharon Binkley-Smith's thorough investigation inside the cab of the Chevy truck was more fruitful. She wrote in her report, "We met Sergeant Roderick at the Office of Emergency Services garage, where he used specialized tools to open a locked passenger door of the cab. Areas on the exterior of the door likely to be disturbed during the forced entry were dusted prior to entry to develop any latent fingerprints. . . . During processing of the exterior surface of the cab, it became apparent that a wide area of the surfaces around the door handle and on the driver's side had been wiped off using broad circular motions. Bloodstains noted on the door sill on the passenger side also showed a pattern of streaks indicative of wiping efforts, possibly to prevent bloodstains from becoming visible from outside.

"Photographs were taken of the interior surfaces of the doors, then of the interior surfaces of the cab. Bloodstains were noted on the interior panel of the driver's door and the dashboard, on papers laid out on top of the dashboard and on the mats. Bloodstains were also noted on the steering wheel and on the gearshift knob. The driver's shoulder/seat belt harness was blood soaked. Blood had run down the belt and covered the seat recliner mechanism and floorboard carpeting directly beneath the belt."

Of all the material at hand she was able to lift a usable print off one of Barbara Muszalski's bloody business cards. It contained the fingerprint of Benjamin Pedro Gonzales.

Binkley-Smith was a trace evidence expert as well. She was able to match small wooden fragments found on the Chevy's floorboard to damaged knives also found in the pickup.

She wrote, "The wood fragments from items #12, 13, and 14 were compared to each other and to the wood handles of knives and forks from items #38 and 39. Wood fragments #12 and 13 correspond to a countersunk screw or rivet that holds the knife blade to the handle."

When Dave Williams was shown the knife found in the cab of Barbara Muszalski's pickup, he identified it as his missing kitchen knife.

The criminalists bit by bit were adding to the detectives' arsenal of clues that linked the murder to Benjamin Gonzales. They were busy as well, hitting the streets and conducting phone interviews. By now they had compiled a list of twelve aliases that Benjamin Gonzales had used:

Robert Gonzales
Ron Gonzales
Santiago Gonzales
Dino Art Cruze
Arthur Cruze
Robert Marino
Juan Reyes
Art Roybal
James Angel
Nick D'Amico
Juan Mario Reyes
Cheeco

They knew he had been in the California cities of Los Angeles, Hollywood, Fresno, Costa Mesa, Simi Valley, San Jose, Campbell—as well as New York City, Chicago, Dallas, Las Vegas and parts of Colorado.

By the end of April, the detectives had a bulletin out to police departments that contained a computer-aided, age-enhanced photograph of Gonzales, based on his old Department of Motor Vehicles driver's license of Dino Art Cruze. As Sergeant Toussaint told a *Valley Times* reporter, "This is just the beginning, not the end of our investigation."

In fact, more clues linking Benjamin Gonzales to the murder of Barbara Muszalski were coming in every day. All of them were necessary if he was ever to be convicted. Karen Tennyson, a Protective Services Officer at the Lawrence Livermore Laboratory, Site 300 on Tesla Road, remembered that at about eight A.M. on April 9, 1992, she saw a Hispanic male in his thirties, about 5'8" and weighing around 160 pounds, walking west on Lupin Way. He was wearing a baseball cap, red-blue-gray plaid shirt, navy blue vest and blue jeans. He had a ponytail. She also lived on Lupin Way and had often seen him walking with his head down, not looking at traffic or anyone. He seemed to be very furtive in his actions.

Sergeant Brian Lerche had also discovered something interesting in the cab of Barbara Muszalski's pickup. It was a bottle of Extra-Strength Maalox Plus with a large "H"—FOR HOSPITAL USE ONLY—stamped on the side. When he asked if any of the Muszalski family members or Dave Williams used Maalox, they all said no. But they knew Gonzales had stomach problems.

Sergeant Lerche investigated the contents of Gonzales's medicine cabinet at the Williams ranch and found several bottles of Maalox. He noted the lot numbers, then contacted Fred Yee at Highland Hospital's pharmacy, who said they got all their lots of Maalox from Berger Brunsburg Drug Company in Sacramento. Sergeant Lerche then contacted the drug company and confirmed that these particular lots could only have been distributed at a hospital. They were not for retail sale.

There was another unforeseen factor causing the Alameda County detectives problems aside from all the aliases that Benjamin Pedro Gonzales used. Unfortunately for them, there was another Benjamin P. Gonzales living in Los Angeles and he had been in trouble with the law as well. On August 11, 1989, he had for no apparent reason attacked Ernie Garcia with a screwdriver on the corner of Glenoaks and Van Nuys Boulevard. Just like the M.O. of the man they sought, the attack was totally unprovoked. This particular Benjamin Gonzales took a dislike to Ernie Garcia and hit him in the face below the right eye. He then pulled a screwdriver out of his jacket and proceeded to chase Garcia into the middle of the street, where they were both nearly hit by a car. But the chase didn't stop there. Gonzales chased Garcia for blocks and didn't give up until Garcia ran into a Church's Chicken outlet.

Gonzales was eventually caught and arrested

and served some time for the attack. But he wasn't Benjamin Pedro Gonzales—he was Benjamin Paul Gonzales. But the similarity of names, locales and type of crime certainly added to the confusion. It was finally ascertained by the Alameda County detectives that they were looking at two distinct individuals and the attack on the corner of Glenoaks and Van Nuys was not perpetrated by their suspect.

Meanwhile, Ivan Meyer at Highland Hospital was certainly aware of "Robert" Gonzales's disappearance from the area. He had seen reports of the crime on television and had no illusions by now that Gonzales was probably involved in the Barbara Muszalski murder. But on June 17, 1992, he was to get a lot more than that. His phone rang and when he picked up the receiver he heard a familiar voice on the other end of the line. It was the voice of Benjamin Gonzales.

"Do you know who this is?" Gonzales asked.

"Yes," Ivan replied.

"Does everyone at Highland Hospital know [about the murder]?" Gonzales asked.

"Yes. We all know."

"Don't believe everything you hear."

Then Gonzales hung up.

A few minutes later he called again. This time he said, "Do you know any places in Arizona where I can receive treatment?"

Meyer answered, "Probably in Tucson or Phoenix."

"I'm feeling very sick and practically blind in one eye. I'm having trouble breathing and pain in my legs. And I got purple [lesions] on my legs. I haven't had medication for a couple of months. I was going to go to a hospital, but I couldn't trust them."

Then he said, "I hope nothing bad comes out of this phone call," and hung up once again.

The implied threat was not lost on Ivan Meyer.

But despite the threat, Ivan called Sergeant Toussaint and told him of the conversation with Gonzales. He said he heard road noises in the background and was sure that Gonzales was calling from a street-side pay phone.

With the prospect that Gonzales was probably out of state and might be in Arizona, the FBI was asked to become involved. FBI Agent Evans was assigned to help in the case on an "Unlawful Flight to Avoid Prosecution" charge.

Gonzales was on the run all right, but he had a dozen known areas to run to and a dozen aliases to hide behind. It was not going to be easy tracking him down.

In July 1992, Sergeant Brian Lerche had a bit of luck. From a phone records search he found that Gonzales's mother, Jenny, had received a phone call from a pay phone at American Transmissions on Del Paso Boulevard in Sacramento, California. The phone call had been made in June. When Sergeant Lerche phoned the transmission shop, he discov-

ered that a former worker named William Lee
Duvall still lived in the area and he was an
ex-boyfriend of Jenny Gonzales.

On July 29, 1992, Sergeant Lerche drove up
to Sacramento and talked with Duvall. What
he found out was both exciting and frustrating.
Benjamin Gonzales had been staying with Duvall for nearly two months after his disappearance from the San Francisco International
Airport parking garage. Only a few days before
Sergeant Lerche arrived, Gonzales had suddenly asked Duvall for a ride to the Greyhound
Bus station in San Jose. Gonzales had found
out that detectives were nosing around the
transmission shop on Del Paso Boulevard. Duvall had let Gonzales off on a street corner several blocks from the bus station. He had the
impression that Gonzales was running from
something.

William Duvall knew Gonzales well. In March
1991, right after the Yvonne Hausley murder
in New York City, Gonzales had suddenly appeared at Duvall's mobile home park in Rio
Linda, a suburb of Sacramento. He stayed with
Duvall and Jenny Gonzales for a few months.
He had told Duvall at the time, "I had to leave
[New York] because I just whacked [killed]
someone."

Duvall thought at the time Gonzales was just
bragging. He was always making stuff up and
it was hard to know what to believe.

After Gonzales left in the summer of 1991
for parts unknown, William Duvall had a stroke
and was hospitalized. Jenny Gonzales moved

out, down to San Jose, and Duvall, once he
was out of the hospital, found a new place to
reside on Del Paso Boulevard near the transmission shop.

Then in mid-April 1992, Benjamin Gonzales
was suddenly once again at his door. He wore
a baseball cap, had a small ponytail and carried
a duffel bag full of clothes. He said he needed
a place to stay. Duvall let him in. Once again,
Duvall had the feeling that Gonzales was running from something. Gonzales made lots of
phone calls from pay phone booths. He
seemed to always have enough money. Duvall
noticed that Gonzales played lottery tickets a
lot. Gonzales would often go down to the
banks of the Sacramento River, not to swim or
fish, but just to stare at the murky waters. He
always was kind of strange in that regard. He
could stare at nothing in particular for hours.

In late July, Gonzales asked Duvall for that
ride to the San Jose bus station, and now here
was Sergeant Lerche telling Duvall of a brutal
murder.

Sergeant Brian Lerche had to curse his luck
for having just missed Benjamin Gonzales in
Sacramento. At least he knew that he was still
on his trail. But as August 1992 rolled around,
the trail grew cold. All the promising leads began to dry up. It seemed that once again Benjamin Pedro Gonzales had fallen right off the
law-enforcement radar. The autumn of 1992
was a series of disappointing leads that tailed
off into nothing.

But Sergeants Toussaint and Lerche were not

giving up. As Sergeant Toussaint had told the *Valley Times* reporter, "This isn't the end of the investigation, but just the beginning." As the leads dried up, the two sergeants turned to more unorthodox means to track Benjamin Pedro Gonzales down. They turned to television.

Six

America's Most Wanted

In early October 1992, Sergeant Brian Lerche contacted the television program *America's Most Wanted* to see if they were interested in doing a segment on Benjamin Gonzales. They weren't—so he turned to *Prime Suspect,* a similar program on another network, and they accepted his offer. On October 9, *Prime Suspect* sent a crew to film on location in Livermore, San Francisco International Airport and Los Angeles. The segment aired nationwide on Saturday, November 9, 1992.

Although many tips came in, there were no helpful clues in California. However, a viewer in New York saw the photo of Benjamin Gonzales and contacted the New York City Police Department. He had known this individual at Show World as Antonio Perillo and he remembered the murder of Yvonne Hausley. Not only did the perpetrator look the same, but the murders were remarkably similar.

For the first time a link was forged between

Benjamin Gonzales and the 1991 murder of
Yvonne Hausley at the Show World Theater.
Up until this point, law enforcement authorities in New York City had no idea that "Perillo" was actually Gonzales. NYPD Detective
Lenny Ferguson agreed that detectives had
been stymied about the Hausley murder until
the *Prime Suspect* show. When Detective Ferguson showed employees at Show World Gonzales's photograph, they said, "Yes," that was
the man they had known as Perillo.

Another NYPD detective deeply involved in
the Hausley murder was Mike Geddes, the veteran of Forty-second Street. Through diligent
investigation, he tracked Perillo/Gonzales's
route from the Show World Theater after the
Hausley murder to the Port Authority bus station, where Gonzales had obtained a bus ticket
to Sacramento, California. Just as William Duvall in Sacramento had said, Gonzales had
shown up at his mobile home park soon thereafter claiming to have "whacked" someone in
New York City.

NYPD Lieutenant Arthur Monihan sought an
indictment against Benjamin Gonzales for the
murder of Yvonne Hausley and now there were
two arrest warrants out for him instead of one.
But things were just getting started for Gonzales as far as television went. Because of the
promising New York leads, *Prime Suspect* aired
another segment on Gonzales on January 7,
1993. By now *America's Most Wanted* was interested as well, and they sent a crew to film in
New York City, San Leandro, Livermore and

Los Angeles, California. Their segment aired nationwide on February 19, 1993, and garnered 275 tips. None were particularly useful in the San Francisco Bay Area or New York, but the program did pique the interest of a Los Angeles Police Department detective named Frank Bolan. The violent murders of Barbara Muszalski and Yvonne Hausley looked an awful lot like a case he'd been on concerning Dondi Johnson. The Dondi Johnson murder had taken place in his own backyard, in fact, only two blocks away from his office on Venice Boulevard. The suspect he was after was variously known as James Angel, Nick D'Amico, or just Ben.

Detective Bolan worked out of the Wilshire Division of the Los Angeles Police Department. It was in the same neighborhood that had once been a fashionable adjunct to the city and home to several movie stars of the silent era. Fatty Arbuckle had owned a house in the neighborhood and so had Buster Keaton. But since that time, it had slowly slid into decline. The one area that had managed to keep up appearances was the neighborhood where Dondi Johnson had been murdered and where lawyer William McKinney resided. It still retained an old-fashioned kind of elegance, if frayed somewhat, as you neared the major boulevards. There, transients roamed the streets and crime was more pervasive.

Detective Frank Bolan looks like a "cops'" cop, with his dark moustache and powerful frame. He wears the revolver on his belt with a veteran's authority. By 1993, he'd been on the LAPD force for twenty-four years—seventeen of them in Homicide. In that time, he'd seen just about everything on the mean streets of L.A. But the savagery of Dondi Johnson's murder had taken even him aback. She had not just been murdered, she'd been slaughtered. That it had been perpetrated on a quiet street virtually around the corner from his office really got under his skin. He made it a personal point to track down the "prime suspect," no matter how long it took. When he saw the segment about the vicious murder of Barbara Muszalski, he thought, "My God, it's just like the Dondi Johnson murder. Same M.O. This guy likes to use a knife and carve up his victims. And all of them are women he fixates on."

In his hunt for the killer, he'd discovered that Angel/Gonzales had been a loan shark enforcer at the Bicycle Club cardroom. He also learned that the suspect had gone to his lawyer's house right after the murder of Dondi Johnson. Detective Bolan already had the full police report about the Johnson murder, as well as the arson investigator's report about the car fire. In his talk with William McKinney, he learned that Gonzales had been given a towel to wipe blood from himself, as well as a change of clothes. He also learned about Gonzales's insistence that they not travel on the 1400 block of Victoria Avenue and the strange route they had taken to Gonzales's apartment on Yucca Street in Hollywood.

But what really made Detective Bolan's ears perk up was a startling revelation by William McKinney. He said that Benjamin Gonzales had told him, either on their ride to Hollywood, or at some later time (and the timing was not clear at this point), "I just killed my girlfriend!"

When asked who the "girlfriend" was, McKinney said that Gonzales had been referring to Dondi Johnson at the time. He had an obsession about her.

There was only one problem with this incredible admission of guilt. Benjamin Gonzales had told McKinney this in confidence. He did crazy things, but he wasn't stupid. He knew that just like a priest, William McKinney could not give evidence against his own client. Anything he told the police now could not be used in a court of law. It was all privileged information.

So this admission was unfortunately inadmissable evidence. If Bolan was going to collar Gonzales for the murder of Dondi Johnson, he was going to have to build up a great deal of circumstantial evidence, or have Gonzales admit the crime to him personally.

LAPD Detective Dan Andrews, who was also working on the case, said, "Benjamin Gonzales is a suspect in Dondi Johnson's murder—the only suspect we've ever had and the only suspect we ever will have. But at present we don't have a fileable case because of a legal technicality." The legal technicality was, of course, the admission to Gonzales's lawyer, McKinney.

They may not have had enough to bring Gonzales to trial because of that technicality, but that wasn't going to keep Detective Bolan from trying. If he couldn't get Gonzales on the confession to his lawyer, then he'd keep on piling up the circumstantial evidence until it was stacked so high he couldn't escape. It wouldn't be easy, but Detective Bolan had a bulldog tenacity and persistence. He figured he owed that much to Dondi Johnson. A killer evading justice did not sit well with him.

There was one unfortunate side effect of Detective Bolan's meeting with McKinney at the time. The lawyer gave him just enough information to set Bolan off in the wrong direction. McKinney wasn't being purposefully evasive, but he walked a tightrope between client-attorney privilege and obstruction of justice. So what he told the detective sent Bolan off on a wild goose chase up in San Jose, California, where Gonzales did indeed have family. While he was there, Detective Bolan contacted fifty different Gonzaleses' residences in an effort to find Benjamin Pedro Gonzales. But most of them weren't related to Ben. What was even worse was that the suspect wasn't near that area at the time.

All of this was frustrating, but Detective Bolan knew it came with the territory. Real breaks generally came after long hours of drudgery and solid police work. It was not easy finding someone who was employing every trick in the book not to be found.

So far the two crime shows had been only marginally helpful in tracking down Benjamin Gonzales. They had alerted the New York Police Department and the Los Angeles Police Department to his real name and his possible connection with their murders, and not much more. But all of that was about to change. On Saturday, April 24, 1993, *Prime Suspect* aired a six-minute segment once again about Gonzales in the Los Angeles area only. It was just a filler segment, something to take up time between other stories. But it had one very important viewer, a man named Ray Battaglia.

Battaglia was stunned when he saw the photo of Gonzales on the television and heard the story. He knew the suspect as "Bobby." But he hadn't heard from him in eight months. Then out of the blue on April 25, the day after the *Prime Suspect* broadcast, Gonzales gave him a call. He said he needed money, a place to stay, new false identifications and a way to get out of the country. Battaglia lied to Gonzales and said he would help. Instead, he attempted to contact law enforcement authorities.

There was only one problem: he hadn't written down the number to call. All he could remember from the telecast was that the murder of one of the victims had taken place in Alameda County. He started calling police departments of cities in that county by alphabetical order—Alameda, Albany, Berkeley, El Cerrito, etc. When he called the Livermore Police Department, they told him they weren't handling the case, but they switched him over to an Alameda County Sheriff's Department watch commander, who contacted Sergeant Brian Lerche.

Sergeant Lerche was at home when he received the phone call from Battaglia. He was pretty blasé when he first took the phone call. He'd already fielded hundreds of tips over the last year, most of them totally useless. But when Battaglia said he knew Gonzales as "Bobby" and the man had just phoned him in an attempt to exit the United States, Sergeant Lerche's skepticism vanished. This was the biggest break he'd had since the case had begun the previous April. He and Sergeant Toussaint had almost caught up with Gonzales in Sacramento at William Duvall's place and had missed him by a matter of a single day. He crossed his fingers that Gonzales would not elude them this time.

Sergeant Lerche made arrangements with the Los Angeles Sheriff's Office Fugitive Unit to set up a trap with the informant involved. It was to be an elaborate ruse to get Gonzales into their custody.

Battaglia called Benjamin Gonzales and made arrangements to meet at San Diego's Aztec Theater, not far from the border of Mexico. Little did Gonzales know that when he exited the theater, his friend wouldn't be waiting outside—Los Angeles County Sheriff's officers of the Fugitive Unit would be there to greet him instead.

As the officers milled around on the sidewalk in front of the Aztec Theater, it was not lost on them that there had been another famous ruse involving a criminal and informant. John Dillinger had been lured to a movie theater by the infamous Lady in Red, and it had ended up in a shootout with Dillinger dead on the sidewalk. They hoped for different results in this case, but they had to be ready for anything.

At exactly twelve-thirty A.M. on April 26, 1993, Benjamin Gonzales warily stepped outside the Aztec Theater after watching *A Far Off Place*. The movie was a tale of two teens running from poachers who have killed their parents in Africa. Chased across the burning sands of the Kalahari Desert, they were aided by a young bushman as they made their desperate escape. They suffered incredible thirst and privations with the constant threat of capture by the poachers. God only knows what thoughts coursed through Gonzales's mind as he watched this movie about being chased. Perhaps he hoped his friend Battaglia would be like the bushman and help him escape. For the teens in the movie, a town on the Atlantic Ocean meant safe haven. For Gonzales, it was Mexico, only a few miles away.

When Gonzales departed the theater, he walked straight into the arms of the Los Angeles County Sheriff's officers. Unlike the Dillinger shootout, everything ended peacefully.

Informed that he was under arrest for the murder of Barbara Muszalski, all the fire went out of Benjamin Gonzales and he surrendered without incident.

Gonzales was taken to the San Diego County Jail, where his identification was verified. Even then he was still trying to be evasive. He said he was Robert Gonzales and then he said his name was Mike Lopez. But law enforcement officers knew they had the one and only Benjamin Pedro Gonzales in custody.

From the initial booking at the county jail, he was transferred to the Central Detention Facility at the San Diego County Sheriff's Department to spend the night. Right at the top of the list of those overjoyed by his capture was Sergeant Brian Lerche. He'd spent more than a year tracking down every lead he could on the whereabouts of Benjamin Gonzales. He told a *Valley Times* reporter, "He'll be a very interesting person to talk to, if he agrees to talk. We don't know what's going on in his head, but if he decides to talk, I'm sure he'll have a lot of things to say."

Sergeant Dale Toussaint was also happy about Gonzales's capture. Even though he'd been transferred off the case to another one, he told the *Tri-Valley Herald*, "Maybe there's a woman somewhere that isn't going to get stabbed to death since he's seemed to make a habit of it."

The Alameda County Sheriff's sergeants

weren't the only ones elated by Gonzales's incarceration. *Prime Suspect* producer Steve Durgin, said, "It's a real charge. It's much better than getting ratings."

Jamie Muszalski, Barbara's daughter, told a *Tri-Valley Herald* reporter, "Tears come to my eyes. And, oh, God, relief. I just didn't expect it. I've been dreading this moment and looking forward to it at the same time."

Jim Muszalski was even more adamant in his sentiments. He said, "Barbara's life and the way she was demanded that this person come to justice. I hope they find him guilty of whatever it takes to have him put to death."

There was another police officer on his way out to San Diego to look into the Gonzales case and he was flying all the way out from New York City. Detective Mike Geddes was sure that Benjamin Gonzales was responsible for the murder of Yvonne Hausley at the Show World Theater. In the past year, he'd looked into every angle of the old case and noticed the same M.O. as the other crimes. Just like with Barbara Muszalski and Dondi Johnson, the stab wounds had a similar pattern on the upper body, the eyes of the victims and one particularly savage wound that extended from the abdomen up to the area of the heart. There were also no sexual encounters with these women. Detective Geddes surmised that these patterns were Gonzales's signature.

That Benjamin Gonzales was a serial killer, Detective Geddes was certain. He stalked women co-workers, he badgered them, and when they spurned his advances, he killed them in the most brutal fashion possible. He'd flown low under the police radar surveillance all these years because of his aliases and ability to change his looks. But Detective Geddes discovered one common thread in all of Gonzales's travels across the country—he always carried a small duffel bag with him. If Geddes could lay his hands on that bag, he was sure he would find items from each of Gonzales's killings. They were, in some twisted way, "trophies" of his exploits. Even though Gonzales wasn't a sexual killer in the classic sense, his murders still had overtones of this type of killer. In some ways, the savage stabbings were a sexual release for him when the situation became unbearable in his mind. And just like these sexual killers, Detective Geddes surmised that Gonzales liked to keep reminders of the murders. As Mauro V. Corvasce and Joseph R. Paglino wrote in *Murder One*, "Souvenir gathering is a common trait among sexual killers because they love to relive the killing. When they are unable to get victims, these souvenirs assist them in suppressing and relieving their desires. When the police search the killers' residences, they usually find these souvenirs, along with newspaper clippings about the killings."

Detective Mike Geddes also had another theory—he didn't believe that Gonzales had committed only the three murders. With all Gonzales's traveling back and forth across the United States and his propensity for violence,

Geddes believed he had killed more people, both men and women. The proof of this probably would be found in the inside of that little duffel bag that went everywhere with Gonzales.

Detective Geddes touched down in San Diego and began an immediate search of Benjamin Gonzales's last known locations. The trail was just about as hard to follow as Gonzales himself had been while he was on the run. But Mike Geddes was a good detective and he followed the trail of the missing duffel bag through southern California to the Mexican border. Then right when he felt he was near the payoff, the authorities above him back in New York City called for his return. Whether they thought he was dogging it in San Diego, looking for any excuse to stay in sunny California instead of rainy New York, or whether they thought he should be back on other cases, they didn't say. Mike Geddes had, after all, just made a big collar in a high-profile case back in New York (the Chippendale case involving the owner of that male stripper establishment), and it was time to start preparing for trial. But he was certain ever after that the missing duffel bag would have presented everyone with valuable clues and evidence. He was also sure that after he was recalled, the bag was "destroyed" by someone other than Gonzales and that it never would be found.

As events would prove later, Detective Mike Geddes was correct in his assessments that Gonzales had killed more people than just

Dondi Johnson, Yvonne Hausley and Barbara Muszalski. The source of that information would come from someone nobody could have guessed at, at the time.

On April 27, 1993, Sergeant John Reasoner, who had taken over Sergeant Dale Toussaint's duties on the case, and Sergeant Brian Lerche flew from Livermore to San Diego in a private jet. At 9:55 A.M., they had their first look at Benjamin Gonzales in the flesh. Sergeant Reasoner said of him, "He was much healthier than we expected him to be. Even slightly overweight—considering he tested HIV positive in July 1991 and had no known source of money to pay for treatment. Our concern was that he was going to die or pass away before we captured him, and he would be buried someplace in a pauper's grave and we wouldn't know it."

When the Alameda Sheriff's sergeants met Gonzales at the San Diego Detention Facility, they explained who they were and read him his rights. Gonzales said he knew his rights, but that he wanted to talk to an attorney, and the interview was terminated.

Gonzales was fairly quiet on his way to Lindbergh Field in San Diego, but once aboard the Beechcraft Ranger for the two-and-a-half-hour flight back to Livermore, he became more talkative. He struck up a conversation with Sergeant Brian Lerche, who was sitting next to him. Gonzales admitted that he'd moved around a lot for over a year trying to evade capture, and that he was glad it was over. He told Sergeant Lerche, "I feel free in a way now."

He then started to talk a lot about organized crime and the FBI. He kept bringing up the name Mike Wax, who he said was an FBI agent in Los Angeles. (Sergeant Lerche could not confirm that name later.) Gonzales said that he had spoken to Agent Wax on several occasions, discussing organized crime in the Los Angeles area. But now he was afraid of both the street gangs and the FBI. He asked Sergeant Lerche, "Are there any federal holds on me?"

Sergeant Lerche answered, "The unlawful flight to avoid arrest charge will probably be dropped."

"That's good," Gonzales said, but he was still afraid of being photographed. "They want to kill me," he said. He didn't explain who the "they" were or why they wanted him dead.

Detective Lerche said, "He had a real fixation about the mafia and the mob. He intimated that he had been part of it, but a lot of what he said seemed doubtful. He seemed prone to fantasizing about this. For some reason, it gave him a charge to think he was mob related. Maybe it had something to do with his self-image. He could be very rational one moment, and then the next his comments were way off the mark."

Gonzales asked, "If there are any photographers at the airport, can you cover my head?"

Sergeant Lerche agreed to cover Gonzales's

head with an extra pair of pants he had in his possession. Then Lerche said, "It would be very interesting to hear what's in your head. You've probably had a very interesting life."

Gonzales leaned over and said, "I'll write you a letter explaining what happened after everything's over." He never did. It was not the first or last time he would promise something and then renege.

Finally Sergeant Lerche told Gonzales that he'd had several conversations with his mother, Jenny.

Gonzales asked how she and the other family members were doing and then said, "Can you contact her again? I don't feel comfortable speaking to her right now."

Sergeant Lerche said that he would.

In fact, Gonzales didn't talk about himself much or what he'd been doing for the last year or where he'd been. He and Detective Lerche mostly talked about various members of Gonzales's family. Benjamin was so relaxed with Detective Lerche at this point that they were on a first-name basis. He became very emotional about his mother and sister and began crying. Detective Lerche thought he might open up about other things related to the case at this point, since his emotions were so near the surface. Detective Lerche was soon to discover that Benjamin Gonzales would go only so far. Lerche said later, "He was crazy like a fox. He knew just how far he could take things. When we were flying into Livermore, we flew directly over the Muszalski ranch. I leaned over and said to him, 'Look down there, that's where you used to live'—just to see what his reaction would be. He totally clammed up and refused to even look at the ranch."

Just as Benjamin Gonzales feared, the Livermore Airport was crawling with reporters and photographers. His capture was a big story in the San Francisco Bay Area. True to his word, Sergeant Lerche draped a pair of pants over Gonzales's head before they departed the plane. It was a very odd sight seeing the short and stocky Gonzales being escorted across the tarmac between two big sheriff's sergeants with a pair of pants over his head. If the photographers couldn't get a photo of his face, they certainly got one of this bizarre sight.

Besides all the journalists, there was one other special person in the crowd—Sergeant Dale Toussaint. He told a *Valley Times* reporter, "Since I'm the one who told Jim Muszalski that we found his wife's body a year ago, I really wanted to be here today."

Less ebullient than the Alameda County Sheriff's officers was Los Angeles Police Department Detective Dan Andrews. He said, "We have a lot of circumstantial evidence [in the Dondi Johnson murder], but his [Gonzales's] statement to his lawyer is the single most critical factor in our investigation. As far as Ben Gonzales coming back to Los Angeles and facing his accusers, I don't think that is going to happen."

Then he added that he hoped Gonzales would cooperate with authorities in Alameda County to help clear up the Dondi Johnson case that had been troubling Andrews for four years.

Even though Gonzales wasn't telling him anything at present, Detective Andrews was at least pleased that he was in custody. But as he was led away in handcuffs toward the Alameda County Jail at Santa Rita, only time would tell if Benjamin Gonzales was willing to cooperate with anybody.

Seven

The Enraged Boy

Benjamin Pedro Gonzales was born on August 31, 1959, in Denver, Colorado. His father, Benjamin Guzman Gonzales, was much older than his mother, Jenny Mary Roybal.

Benjamin did not have a happy childhood. It was a chaotic household right from the beginning, with more and more children on the way until Ben eventually had nine other brothers and sisters, according to one source. The same source intimated that not all of them were "in wedlock."

According to Benjamin, his father was strict to the point of mental and physical abuse. He would claim later at his trial, "My father used to tie me up and beat me and stuff. He tied me up for nineteen days one time. He'd beat me with a belt and other things. [It] left scars—his scars."

He would also recall at his trial, "One time when he tied me up and beat me, I felt at peace. I could hear my mother calling me, and

I knew then that if I could hear 'my' voice, I could go back into the light, and I don't have to be here."

For Benjamin, his mother represented the "good light," while his father represented the "dark light." He made no bones about having affection for his mother, while he harbored a hatred and dread of his father. Just about anything he did seemed to set the elder Gonzales off. Even though Ben was generally quiet spoken and could appear meek at times, his father had a towering rage when it came to the boy. Nothing Ben did seemed to satisfy him, and at those times he would be punished for even insignificant transgressions.

Ben also intimated later about sexual abuse at home. He never specified whether it was by his father or someone else, but the message was clear: he had been molested as a boy. He said, "When I was a child, when I used to go to people and tell them about my father . . . there were a couple of men [who heard this] and wanted to sexually abuse me. When I told other people, they didn't want to hear it. They would say something to my father and I'd be tied to a post and whipped again."

The abuse was apparently so bad that Benjamin began to escape into a fantasy world. He claimed later on that even in childhood he began to hear voices and experience multiple personalities. He called the voices "spirits." They not only spoke to him of other realities, they let him escape from traumas, both real and imagined.

The corporal abuse of Benjamin Gonzales left not only physical scars, but emotional ones as well. It's been noted by psychiatric agencies that physically abused children have a hard time as adults in establishing intimate personal relationships. They have problems with closeness, touching, intimacy and trust. They are also at high risk for anxiety, depression and substance abuse.

According to the American Academy of Child and Adolescent Psychiatry, these children of abuse are prone to a poor self-image, inability to trust or love others, aggressive, disruptive and illegal behavior, self-destructive behavior, school problems, drug and alcohol abuse and anger and rage. Benjamin Gonzales would go on to display aspects of all these factors as an adult.

Reports note that such abused children often have sleep problems and nightmares, as well as secretiveness and withdrawal from others. They may create their own fantasy world. Benjamin Gonzales became secretive to the extreme, even as to go so far as to constantly change his name and not use a last name around people. It was as if he wanted to be removed from himself. Many people he met later in life knew him only as "Bobby," "Art," "Cheeco," "Nick," "Santiago" or "Tony."

The need to disassociate himself from his pain eventually led to a kind of Post Traumatic Stress Disorder, where he sought a state of emotional numbness to block out bitter memories. But he had problems containing his an-

ger, and the spillover resulted in lashing back
at the world. He became a master at stealing
and lying—even at an early age. The stealing
made a certain amount of twisted sense in his
mind. According to the American Academy of
Child and Adolescent Psychiatry, "Children
who repeatedly steal may also have difficulty
trusting others and forming close relationships.
Rather than feeling guilty, they may blame the
behavior on others, arguing, 'Since they refuse
to give me what I need, I will take it.' "

Benjamin Gonzales needed a lot by the time
he was an adolescent. He had an emotional
and moral vacuum created by all the physical
and emotional punishment his father had be-
stowed upon him. He still respected his
mother, but not even she had been able to protect him. If he couldn't count on her, he
couldn't count on anybody. He was a time
bomb ready to explode.

By his teenage years, Benjamin Gonzales was
enrolled in high school in Campbell, California. But he never cared much for learning or
classroom discipline. He exclaimed later, "I
hated school. I hated the teachers. They reminded me of my father."

To add to all his woes, Benjamin began ex-
perimenting with drugs. He smoked marijuana
and later claimed to have tried LSD. With its
well-known knack for creating vivid hallucinations and distorting time and space, LSD al-
tered Gonzales's already tenuous grasp on

reality. He liked to "party," but his parties meant getting high by himself. He was generally a loner, and LSD use added to his sense of isolation.

Even more potent and disorienting for Benjamin Gonzales's world was his use of PCP. Popular among certain groups of drug users in the late 1970's and early 1980's, PCP was, in effect, an animal tranquilizer. Officially named phencyclidine, it had been invented in 1959 as an anesthetic for veterinarians. Known by its street names—angel dust, angel hair or mist—it generally came to the user as a white powder, or a tablet, or a liquid that could be sprayed on marijuana joints. It could be swallowed, sniffed, smoked or injected.

Habitual users said that PCP gave them feelings of strength, power and invulnerability. During its use they experienced a rise in blood pressure and pulse. Flushing and sweating, they suffered muscle discoordination, just like the effects of severe alcoholic intoxication. But it also kept them from feeling pain while high. PCP has a numbing effect on the mind and memory—something Gonzales was very aware of. One of his chief aims was to blot out painful memories of childhood beatings by his father, and the realization that his life was not going in the direction he had hoped for. In his case, the absence of memory was bliss.

The effects of PCP can be so strong that a person using it may often not recognize his own body parts. In the throes of a PCP high, abusers might cut or damage parts of their own bodies. Benjamin Gonzales would later admit to cutting himself. He called it, "Doing surgery on myself."

Even worse for Gonzales, PCP users were prone to sudden outbursts of anger and rage—something he was storing in abundance. Often described as quiet, or even meek, he could fly into a towering rage at the drop of a hat. He would refer to himself later as "The Enraged Boy."

One story in particular underscores this sudden and unprovoked rage. Officer Brian Lerche, looking into Gonzales's past, heard about an incident from an acquaintance of Gonzales, who said that one day they were walking down the sidewalk and another man approached them. Neither he nor Gonzales knew the man. But suddenly, for no apparent reason, Benjamin Gonzales "went crazy" and "Sunday punched" the unsuspecting pedestrian. There was no rhyme or reason for the attack. Gonzales did it on some inexplicable impulse.

Moderate doses of PCP were bad enough—but Benjamin Gonzales wasn't moderate about anything in his life. With increased use, he suffered blurred vision, nausea, dizziness and hallucinations. The side effects of PCP mimicked schizophrenia, and Gonzales was already a borderline case. He began to complain about hearing voices and seeing visions. The line between reality and fantasy became so blurred that at times he could not tell which world he was in. In the realm of relationships, especially with women, the line ceased to exist at all.

Whatever delusions he had about a certain woman or girl became his "reality."

By 1978, Ben had had enough of high school and dropped out without getting a diploma. It was the beginning of a string of low-paying jobs and an intinerant life-style that would be the norm for him for every year that he was out of jail. He moved to Los Angeles and lived a very chaotic life there. He had big plans about making it in Hollywood, but parking cars and living on the street were his true fate.

According to Alameda County Inspector Kathy Boyovich, a law enforcement agent who would know Benjamin Pedro Gonzales very well in the years to come, he then met a six-teen-year-old girl that he fell for. This was a story that Ben told others in southern California. The girl soon returned his affection and became "his girlfriend." He created an entire romantic fable about their relationship. He couldn't do enough for her and vice versa. The only problem was that he was older than she and lived a rough life. Her parents did not approve of him and spoke ill of him. But she would not listen to them at first and moved in with Gonzales.

Somewhat later the story changed. She became upset at his temperamental mood swings and started talking back to him. She began listening to the negative comments her parents made about him. In his mind she became a "bitch."

Suddenly and abruptly, he quit talking about

her altogether, just as he would do with Dondi
Johnson and then Yvonne Hausley after he
murdered them. In fact, this pattern was so
pronounced that Inspector Boyovich did not
discount the story gleaned from Gonzales's acquaintances about the sixteen-year-old girl. Inspector Boyovich could never get an exact
name for her, but she believed that the girl
did exist. Perhaps Gonzales and the girl were
never intimate sexually or even romantically.
But it was enough for her to become a fixation
in Gonzales's mind. When she started backing
away from him, he did what he did with all
the women who rejected him—he killed her.
Boyovich believes that Gonzales murdered the
girl and dumped her body somewhere in
southern California. Even if her body was later
found, she was probably chalked up as a Jane
Doe—just another runaway whose life had
turned out badly. There was no connection to
Benjamin Gonzales. He probably used an alias
with her. The sixteen-year-old girl fell through
the cracks of the legal system and became one
more ghostly victim in Benjamin Gonzales's
trail of violent murder.

Sometime after this incident, Gonzales was
back in northern California in search of em-
ployment. Strangely enough, the search led
him to a mortuary in San Jose. Even more
strangely, it lead him to Raul Arredondo, Dave
Williams of Livermore's half brother.

In the early 1980's, Arredondo owned a mortuary in San Jose, California, and Benjamin
Gonzales was one of his employees. Generally

quiet and even a little shy, Benjamin could have a volatile temper on occasions. Raul Arredondo learned about that first hand.

At eight P.M. one day in 1983, Raul was at home when he received a phone call from Benjamin Gonzales. Gonzales said that he needed seventy-five dollars right away, but Raul told him he didn't have it and hung up.

Within minutes, the phone rang again with Gonzales on the line, and he said he was desperate.

"No!" Arredondo snapped, and hung up again.

This phone tag went on two more times with the same results. By the fifth time, Gonzales was furious. He yelled into the phone, "Nobody hangs up on me! You better start making your own funeral arrangements!"

"Flake off!" Arredondo replied and hung up again.

Gonzales called back a sixth time and swore, "I'm on my way and you're dead!"

About thirty minutes later, true to his word, Gonzales showed up at Raul Arredondo's home and kicked in the door. He screamed at Arredondo, "No one hangs up on me!" and produced a knife.

Raul Arredondo had a guest over at the time and that person tried to calm Gonzales down. But Gonzales shouted, "This is none of your business. Get out!"

Then Gonzales turned to Arredondo and said, "Give me the money or I'll kill you."

The guest responded, "I'm calling the police."

But Raul Arredondo knew by Gonzales's expression there was no time for that. He said, "No, I'll give him the money."

He dug into his wallet, gave Benjamin Gonzales the cash and the ruckus was over. Satisfied that he'd made his point, Gonzales left quietly without further comment.

The next day, Benjamin Gonzales showed up for work as usual, as if nothing had happened. But Raul Arredondo did not trust him after that. Unfortunately, he did not relate this story to his half brother, rancher Dave Williams.

Arredondo began to watch Gonzales more closely at work now. At times, Gonzales could be meek and gentle, and at other times violent and aggressive. Arredondo thought Gonzales must be schizophrenic. He noticed that the other co-workers were becoming afraid of Gonzales. He also noticed that Gonzales had obsessive habits and was paranoid. When talking to people, he always wanted to be away from crowds. Often he would speak almost in a whisper. Arredondo began to wonder if Gonzales was wanted by the police.

Before he could find out, Benjamin Gonzales simply disappeared. Arredondo was relieved. In 1987, Raul Arredondo was walking down Hollywood Boulevard showing some of his relatives the sights, when he bumped into Benjamin Gonzales on the street quite by chance. When he asked Gonzales what he was doing there,

Ben answered, "I'm a male prostitute. I hustle on Santa Monica and Hollywood boulevards."

He seemed to be quite pleased with himself. "I can make a lot of money," he said. "I know some movie stars who pay me real well for sex."

Whether they were men or women, he didn't say. At first, Arredondo wondered if this was true or not. But, in fact, this sort of thing wasn't so far-fetched. In the film *Star Maps* a young Hispanic male named Carlos, who was about Benjamin Gonzales's age, hustled on Hollywood's streets to survive. Ostensibly selling maps on the streets that showed the locations of the homes of Hollywood movie stars, his real job was that of a male prostitute. He serviced lonely tourists, bored businessmen and women, and a television soap star who called on Carlos whenever she needed a "sex fix" because of his youth and "staying power."

In all Gonzales's bragging to Raul Arredondo about the money he was making and the Hollywood stars he was having sex with, he failed to mention one other thing. He had been in trouble with the law, and it had started right after he left high school and years before he had even met Arredondo. Significantly enough, his scrapes with the law started right in downtown Hollywood.

On May 10, 1979, Gonzales was arrested for disorderly conduct and prostitution. He was convicted and sentenced to six months' probation and fifty hours of community service. And with the arrest he set a pattern he was to maintain for years to come as far as the authorities were concerned. He gave a false name when asked who he was. Nothing identifying him as Benjamin Pedro Gonzales went into the records. He had so many fake I.D.s that he could pull them out at will. As far as misdemeanors went, the law enforcement agencies didn't dig any deeper to find out if he might be lying about his identity. Even with this first conviction, Gonzales was flying under the law enforcement radar.

On June 30, 1980, he was in trouble with the law again in Los Angeles. The charge was "Conspiracy to solicit specified criminal acts." Just what these acts were has become obscured with time and the loss of bureaucratic paperwork. The authorities didn't even bother sending him to court for his violation. Once again, no record of his real name surfaced on this charge. It was only much later, when he was accused of three murders, that law enforcement officers would even dig up this information.

Gonzales disappeared from clear view after the 1980 incident, and where he was and what he was doing became lost in a murky haze, mostly because he liked it that way. He phoned members of his family on occasion, especially his mother, and he always seemed to be able to find her, even though she moved around a lot, just as he did. But even with her, he would not discuss where he worked, or what he was doing. He would tell a newspaper reporter much later that he started working for organized crime about this time. But this "organized crime" was strictly on a small scale, meaning street gangs, of which there were an abundance in Los Angeles in the 1980's.

In fact, in the 1980's, street gang violence seemed to spring up on every corner of Los Angeles, with violent clashes over drugs and turf. It reminded old-timers of the Prohibition era in Chicago. Except this time, drugs, not bootleg booze, were the source of all the trouble.

Benjamin Gonzales only reemerged from the fog in the summer of 1984 because he was arrested once again in Los Angeles. He didn't reemerge under his real name, but rather another alias that would later be traced back to him. Gonzales attempted to destroy insured property (just what it was also becomes obscured by time and lost paperwork, though rumors are that it was an automobile), for purposes of collecting the insurance money. He was convicted and sentenced to 314 days in the county jail and probation.

Another take on this, according to Inspector Kathy Boyovich, is that the vehicle in question was not a car at all, but a trailer that Gonzales was trying to sell, even though he didn't own it. Something went wrong with the deal, and for some reason, Gonzales set the trailer on fire and was caught. He was convicted, sentenced and served his time in the county jail.

So far it had been all penny-ante crimes for Benjamin Gonzales. But he was just about to advance to the big leagues. His drug use, rough street life, gang affiliation and anger all combined to tip him over the edge. On March 23, 1984, he got into an altercation with a man named Jewel (*sic*) Jubert in Hollywood. This time he didn't use his fists—he pulled out a knife. By the time he was done stabbing Mr. Jubert, the man was a bloody mess and lucky to be alive.

Jewel Jubert was lucky in another way; the police were soon called and Officer Bustos arrested Benjamin Gonzales for "assault by force and with a deadly weapon." Hauled down to the Hollywood Police Station, he was in real trouble this time. Once again, he lied to the authorities as to his name, this time using the alias Santiago Gonzales.

Ordered to a hearing in a municipal court, he was assigned public defender, T. MacBride. Asked how he pleaded in the assault, Gonzales said, "Not guilty." Bail was set at $12,000 and the case was sent on to the Los Angeles Superior Court.

But on June 11,1984, Benjamin Gonzales did something that was to have future ramifications, not only for him but another party as well. He dismissed his court-appointed attorney and hired private practice lawyer William McKinney—the same McKinney near whose home he would butcher Dondi Johnson five years later.

William McKinney, in the case of assault with a deadly weapon used on Jewel Jubert, kept asking the court for more time in the preparation of his case. On June 29, he wrote up a list of items he wanted from the police and prosecution. These included all oral and written statements and admissions by Gonzales, all statements by witnesses, results of all lab tests by the scientific investigation unit of the LAPD and eleven other categories. By December 1984, he was still at it, citing that he had to perform witness checks.

But despite all the delays and information gathering, McKinney knew one thing as the year was ending. The evidence the prosecution had was pretty overwhelming and Benjamin Gonzales's chances in a jury trial did not look good. He sat his client down and advised him to plead guilty and hope for the best.

In the end, McKinney's advice to Gonzales was good. He'd already laid some groundwork with the prosecutor, Richard Size, about such a possibility. They'd discussed terms and McKinney was sure that this was about the best that Gonzales was going to get.

Research had alerted the authorities that Santiago Gonzales was not his real name. So on December 26, 1984, Benjamin Gonzales sat before Judge Clarence Stromwell at the Los Angeles Superior Court and was asked a simple question by the judge that for once he answered truthfully. The judge asked, "Ben Gonzales—is that your true name?"

Stepping out from behind all the murkiness and lies, Benjamin Gonzales replied, "Yes, sir."

He couldn't have known at the time that this simple statement would put down on paper and into the computers documentation that would have an adverse effect upon him later.

It would match his real name to a valid
photo—the police mugshot, and both of these
would go into the California Criminal Record
System. Even though he would lie and fool
people later as to who he actually was, for this
one moment he would emerge through the fog
and be caught in the full glare of the law enforcement apparatus. He would never be able
to erase this moment.

Prosecutor Richard Size asked Gonzales, "Do
you want to plead guilty?"

Gonzales said quietly, "Yes, sir."

The prosecutor told him that he had the
right to face his accusers and a jury trial, and
he was giving all that up by pleading guilty.

Gonzales said he understood.

Size declared, "Assault with a deadly weapon
is a felony. It is punishable by two, three or
four years in the state prison. Your attorney
and I have discussed this case, and because of
your lack of a prior record, the judge has
agreed to sentence you to two years in the state
prison. That's the law."

Whether Benjamin Gonzales was laughing
up his sleeve at all of them is not recorded.
He was getting off lightly because there was no
record of his past offenses and violent nature.
No one knew of these since he'd always been
arrested under an alias, and no authorities
traced those crimes to this present incident. It
wasn't that they were sloppy; it was that he was
that good about covering up his identity. He
truly was a chameleon, able to blend into the
background and escape notice when he wanted

to. He had so many good, authentic-looking fake I.D.s that he had slipped through the walls of justice as if they were a sieve.

Nonetheless, they had him now under his true name, and prosecutor Size asked, "Do you understand that after your release from state prison you will be on probation?"

"Yes, sir," Gonzales answered.

"The terms could include one year in county jail. If you violate the terms you could be sentenced to state prison for four years. So, do you plead guilty freely and voluntarily?"

Gonzales's answer was short and to the point. "Yes."

In California, there is an inmate classification system and inmates are given points for their various behavior patterns and the seriousness of their crimes. They receive points for commitment offenses, unfavorable behavior, background factors and prior incarceration behavior factors. The inmate can also have points taken away for favorable behavior. A score of zero to eighteen will land an inmate in a Level 1 prison, nineteen to twenty-seven in a Level 2 facility, twenty-eight to fifty-one in a Level 3, and fifty-one plus in a Level 4 prison. Level 1 are institutions and camps that consist primarily of open dormitories with a relatively low security perimeter. Level 4 are the worst, with inside cell construction, a secure perimeter and armed coverage. Chino State Prison was a Level 1 facility.

* * *

Benjamin Gonzales could have been sent to
the California Medical Facility at Vacaville by dis-
cretion of the judge. Vacaville in the California
State Prison system was set up to evaluate how
much security a prisoner might need, as well as
ascertain his mental condition. Since Gonzales
had not been seen as violent, except for the
Jewel Jubert stabbing, he was not deemed particularly dangerous. But if he had been sent to
Vacaville, the prison psychologists might have
picked up on the rage that burned beneath the
surface of his quiet exterior. They would have
given him a mental test that would have at least
delved somewhat into his state of mind.

But Vacaville is five hundred miles from Los
Angeles and incredibly overcrowded. Drug offenders rubbed elbows with killers, sex offenders and burglars—all awaiting their turns for
evaluation. It was determined that it would be
much easier and more prudent just to send
Gonzales over the hill to Chino State Prison in
southern California.

Chino Prison was originally known as the
"Prison Without Walls." It had more of a camp
atmosphere to it than a tough prison like Folsom or San Quentin. Gonzales apparently
didn't cause much trouble there. Later reports
would not say much about his incarceration.
He served his time quietly and was released at
the agreed upon time.

* * *

If Gonzales's life before being sent to Chino was murky, the years after his release up until 1989 were downright obscure to the point of a vanishing act. Only bits and pieces of stories come through to illuminate these dark years. Some of the stories were of his own devising, and have to be taken with a grain of salt. Others come from acquaintances and are tinged with their own discrepancies. What is for certain is that Benjamin Gonzales was once again trying to draw the veil of secrecy over himself.

He appears to have gone to Las Vegas for a while. While there, he apparently worked as a loan shark and mixed with the gambling crowd. He claimed to work for organized crime while in Las Vegas. In that capacity, he said he was told to eliminate a man who failed to pay up on his debts. It was to be a warning to others. Gonzales claimed to have killed the man, but the story becomes jumbled at that point. In one retelling, he claimed to have shot the man. In another, to have stabbed him to death. That Benjamin Gonzales could have killed someone is beyond doubt, but whether he killed someone in Las Vegas has not been proven. According to him, he started playing both sides of the fence at this point—working for the mob, but also as a contact for the FBI. He said he became a valuable tool in their arsenal against people higher up the chain. It sounds like a flight of fantasy, but with Gonzales one never knew. After all, he wasn't Benjamin Gonzales anyway to the people who knew him. He was posing under some name so obscure that it becomes lost to legal records at this point.

Some time after this, he moved to Dallas, Texas. He became involved in an export business with an Asian man. Everything there was not on the up and up. There seems to have been trafficking in stolen goods and contraband. The owner was apparently just as free and easy with the law as Gonzales. There was definitely no honor among thieves. Gonzales said later he was about to rip off the owner big time when the man absconded with all the money, leaving his creditors and employees, including Gonzales, high and dry.

During these years, Gonzales was a frequent traveler on Greyhound. He criss-crossed the country several times in search of work and illegal activities. Former New York Detective Mike Geddes seems to think he may have been up to other more dangerous activities as well. He noted Gonzales's frequent and repeated M.O. of falling for women, being rejected by them and then murdering them. He believes it started during this period and that there were other murder victims besides Dondi Johnson, Yvonne Hausley and Barbara Muszalski. Gonzales had a way of slipping in and out of places and just disappearing after committing murder. Detective Geddes would not be surprised if in some small town or large city in America there were other female victims of Gonzales's savagery. The difference compared to the other three is that these victims never came to light. There was no *Prime Suspect* or

America's Most Wanted segment about them. Just like Dondi Johnson and Yvonne Hausley, their names weren't even mentioned in the newspapers. Those two had the unfortunate circumstance of being murdered in large cities, and their deaths were ignored by the media, unlike Barbara Muszalski's, whose death came in a small town. Mike Geddes believes that other women's deaths at Gonzales's hands may have just been chalked up by the local police as yet more unsolved murders. More than ever he regretted not having obtained the duffel bag Benjamin Gonzales always carried with him.

Benjamin Gonzales's actual activities don't come to light again until his work at the Bicycle Club in 1988. In this incarnation he did his work for an Asian street gang. As Mauro Corvasce and Joseph Paglino, investigators for the Prosecutor's Office in Monmouth County, New Jersey, wrote in their book *Murder One*, "Asian street gangs are generally based in the Chinatown sections of large cities. Whether they be Vietnamese, Chinese, Cambodians or others, they are typically spin-offs or branches of larger organized Asian gang families. These types of street gangs typically serve the more established Asian gang families as drug couriers, numbers runners, enforcers and extortion collectors. Asian gang members often just walk up to a noncomplying victim and shoot her and everyone else who may be unfortunate enough to be a witness. . . . It is important to remember their (Asian victims) fear of the police and government. In our country, offenders have a right to bail. In a communist state, the only way to get out of jail is to bribe or cooperate with the officials. So being released on bail in the United States makes it look like the gang has the cooperation of the police, so the gang members go back to the victims and tell them that the reason the gangsters are out is because they have the police under control, just like in their homeland."

There was just one twist to this whole affiliation with Asian gangs as far as Benjamin Gonzales was concerned. He was even more violent than they were. In his role as enforcer and debt collector, he was only supposed to intimidate the mark. After all, it's hard for the person to pay up if he has broken arms or legs and can't work. But Gonzales liked fighting and he liked breaking legs. According to reporter David Holbrook, Gonzales's "boss" in southern California was afraid of him. Gonzales not only wanted to break bones, he wanted to kill someone. He once told his superior in the chain of command, "Let me whack the guy."

Inspector Kathy Boyovich concurred about this violent streak of Gonzales. She said, "His boss was terrified of Gonzales because of his sudden and unexpected rages. He never knew what might set Ben off. In fact, Gonzales stole his boss's car and refused to return it. The guy was too frightened of Ben to press charges or do anything about it in less legal terms. Gonzales was a loose cannon always ready to explode."

While Benjamin Gonzales's life was going nowhere in southern California, the same could not be said for Dondi Johnson. It was true she had a young child to take care of and was a single mom. But by the late 1980's, her life was on an upswing. She moved across the Los Angeles River to the city of Paramount. The Los Angeles River may have not looked like much, especially in the summertime when it was no more than just a large concrete culvert—but it was a dividing line, both physically and psychologically. The west side of the river was poor, rundown and ridden with crime. The east side was more upscale, with a promise of better things to come. Dondi was now on the east side.

She enrolled in Cerritos College, where she took up theater and dance. Even though she didn't excel in anything, other students there remembered her as a pleasant young woman with a lot of charm. It took some of them by surprise when she decided to run for the student senate in the early part of 1989. The school newspaper, the *Talon Marks,* reported that a field of fifty-seven hopeful politicians were vying for thirty open spots in the Associated Students of Cerritos College (ASCC) Senate. They were given a short orientation about student government by the ASCC Court.

As the *Talon Marks* reported, it was more

than just a popularity contest. Phillip House-
man, associate dean of student activities, told
the newspaper, "Spring is an important time
for the student senate. They will be faced with
budgeting nearly half a million dollars for the
1989–90 school year."

Dondi Johnson already knew about finances
and budgeting on a much more personal level.
She had to keep a budget not only for herself
and school, but for her young child as well. In
that quest for more money, she became a
"chip girl" at the Bicycle Club. She counted
on tips from winning gamblers, as well as her
regular salary. But one thing she didn't count
on was meeting up with Benjamin Pedro Gonzales—or as she knew him, James Angel.

Even though Angel (Gonzales) was bugging
her a lot by the second week of February 1989,
she had to have been pleased to be elected to
the student senate at Cerritos College. She
came in near the top of the list as far as voting
went.

But when it came time to take her place on
the senate, when they were voting on extending money to the Criminal Justice Competition
Teams' upcoming trip to the Criminal Justice
Association National Competitions in Rich-
mond, Virginia, she wasn't there to be part of
it. By then she was dead.

Eight

"I Had Him Set Up All Day"

Benjamin Pedro Gonzales began his long ordeal with the justice system on April 28, 1993, at the Livermore–Pleasanton Municipal Court. Dressed in jail-issue clothing, he continually hid his face from journalists' cameras, even though his mugshot had been depicted in every newspaper and on every television station in the area. He covered his face with a blue, jail-issue T-shirt throughout his arraignment in municipal court. He covered his face so well, in fact, that he could barely see where he was going. He actually bumped into the glass partition while making his way to the window where inmates stood before the judge as he addressed them. It got so bad that an Alameda County Sheriff's deputy had to lead him around like a child.

Judge Ronald Hyde was not amused by Gonzales's bizarre performance. He asked how

Gonzales pleaded in the charges against him for the murder of Barbara Muszalski, which included an enhancement for the use of a knife in the killing. Gonzales did not enter a plea, as he awaited the assignment of a defense attorney. Judge Hyde postponed his hearing until this could be arranged. Gonzales was then led, stumbling away, by the sheriff's deputy. It was just a foretaste of things to come.

Back in court two days later, he obtained counsel, while once again covering his face with his hands. He pleaded not guilty.

Judge Hyde stated, "I order that Mr. Gonzales be held to answer to the Superior Court of Alameda to the same [charge], that he be admitted to the same, no bail. It has been ordered that the defendant report to Department 11 of the said Superior Court at nine A.M."

Gonzales was such a difficult inmate that he was held in a maximum security cell, away from the other inmates. He did not eat with the general population, but took his meals in his own cell. He often babbled to himself and yelled at other prisoners who happened to be in the area. Gonzales, ever the loner, did not make friends there. In fact, he soon held a grudge against several other inmates and guards.

In the months before July 1993, all the pretrial machinations were well underway. Both *America's Most Wanted* and *Prime Suspect* wanted to have their cameras allowed in the courtroom to film the proceedings, but Gonzales's court-appointed attorney, Howard Harplan, objected. Judge J. Lewis agreed with the defense, but he did allow still cameras from the *Tri-Valley Herald* and *Valley Times* to be admitted.

On another score, defense attorney Harplan was even more successful. The prosecutor in the case, Deputy D.A. Phil Vaughns, realizing that Gonzales had already created mischief at the Santa Rita County Jail, requested that Gonzales be shackled in the courtroom. He cited not only a danger to those around him, but to everyone in the courtroom, including jurors. Judge Lewis weighed the issue of courtroom safety versus the rights of the accused to a fair trail, and came down on the side of a suspect's rights. Deputy D.A. Vaughns's request was denied.

The D.A.'s office was definitely busy from April 1993 to July of that year. They compiled a list of incriminating photos of the victim, Barbara Muszalski, her pickup and Dave Williams's ranch. They also had a list of witnesses lined up and ready to go, including Jim Muszalski, Dave Williams, RFD mail carrier Katherine Cleek, pathologist Dr. Paul Herrmann, criminalist Kurtis Smith, and fingerprint expert Raquel Craft.

But the defense attorney was also busy compiling evidence to poke holes in the D.A.'s arguments and asking for a motion to dismiss. On July 15, 1993, Benjamin Gonzales spent almost the entire day in the Livermore–Pleasanton Municipal Court as Judge Joseph Hurley decided if there was enough evidence for him

to stand trial at Oakland's Superior Court.
There were more than twenty friends and family members of the Muszalski family there to
see him. But they didn't get to see much. For
more than six hours Gonzales hid his face behind a T-shirt.

Some thought it was a travesty of justice.
Others were glad not to look at his face. Jim
Muszalski was in the latter group. He told a
Valley Times reporter, "I was almost glad he did
it because I was dreading the idea of looking
at him face-to-face again."

Barbara Muszalski's daughter, Jamie, said,
"Listening to some of the evidence was very
difficult. But I wasn't intimidated by him whatsoever and I think that's a really good thing."

One person not amused by Gonzales' T-shirt
shenanigans was Joi Johnson—the mother of
Dondi Johnson. She had come up from Los
Angeles just to see Gonzales in person. She
told a *Tri-Valley Herald* reporter, "The fact that
you could mutilate somebody and leave them
and then cover your face . . . I got so angry.
I found myself jumping out of my chair when
he came in."

She spent the rest of the day teary eyed as
evidence was presented about the knifing and
burning of her daughter's body.

Another person who thought the T-shirt over
the face business was absurd was Alameda
County Sheriff's Sergeant Brian Lerche. "Gonzales did it because he was afraid of the mob,"
he said. "But his photo had been seen all over
the place in newspapers and on television, so

what he was doing now didn't make a whole lot of sense."

One of the most stricken members of the audience present was rancher Dave Williams. He still blamed himself for allowing Gonzales to stay at his Lupin Way ranch. He told the *Valley Times* reporter, "Nobody really knew anything until it was too late. I was starting to get the feeling that this guy was real trouble when this horrible thing happened. The night before they disappeared, she called me to say how he was pushing her to run away with him. She was scared, and I can't get over the fact that if I didn't allow [him] into my house, none of this would have happened."

The evidence given by coroner Dr. Paul Herrmann did not make Dave Williams feel any better. As Dr. Herrmann described all the stab wounds to the body of Barbara Muszalski, the gathered friends and family gasped and shuddered. Some began to cry. Barbara's mother, Marie Schlick, hid her face behind a handkerchief.

Benjamin Pedro Gonzales was hiding his face too—behind his T-shirt. No one could say whether he was crying, smiling or totally oblivious to the proceedings. One thing was for certain though—he couldn't have been happy when Judge Hurley decided that there was indeed enough evidence present for him to stand trial in Oakland Superior Court for the murder of Barbara Muszalski.

* * *

One delay after another postponed the trial as Attorney Harplan requested more time to prepare his defense. Around Christmas 1993, Benjamin Gonzales complained of pain in his right lung, but he refused to be examined if a deputy was present. The whole thing may have been little more than his hopes of a chance to escape. That he was working and plotting toward something unusual became very evident in April 1994.

For over a month, he and the inmate in adjoining cell number 10, Darrell Oliver, had been having words. What started out as taunts and curses turned into full-fledged shouting matches as time progressed. It appeared on the surface that if they ever did tangle, Gonzales would get the worst of it. He was only 5'7", while Oliver was 5'11" and muscular. Besides, Gonzales also suffered from being HIV positive. But Benjamin Gonzales was as cunning as he was persistent.

On April 15, 1994, Darrell Oliver was allowed to take his shower as usual, while Gonzales was left in his cell. Oliver lathered up and was busy scrubbing himself, but Gonzales was busy too. He'd glued an empty milk carton to the wall and folded down the edges so it hid the contents inside. Beneath the folded edges was a tool he had constructed from a black plastic prison comb. It was one inch in length and had all the teeth removed. Along its length it was scored with striations from being jammed in his cell door in an attempt to defeat the sensor-light housing control. On

April 15, he jammed it one more time into the door and this time it worked. His little homemade device effectively fooled the door sensor mechanism, and the jailers had no way of knowing if he was in his cell or not.

Sneaking down the hallway, he could plainly hear the water running in the shower area. He stole up on the unsuspecting Darrell Oliver, wearing only a towel around his waist. When Oliver's back was turned, Gonzales rushed into the shower and hit him in the head. Oliver never saw it coming. He went down, and Gonzales began pummeling him for all he was worth. He beat him so badly that blood began running down the drain. Before long, the whole shower compartment was splattered with blood.

Deputy Chavez and Deputy Lewis were in the area and heard the commotion coming from the shower room and were absolutely stunned to find a naked Gonzales leaning over an equally naked Darrell Oliver, both men awash in a pool of blood. By this time Gonzales was biting the stricken inmate, trying to infect him with the AIDS virus. As the deputies pulled Gonzales off Oliver, he shouted at the prone inmate, "I had you set up all day, mother-fucker!"

Darrell Oliver was taken to Highland Hospital in Oakland, where he was attended to by Nurse Naomi Harrada. She treated his eyes first. The left one was so damaged that it was swollen shut. She next worked on Oliver's bloodied lips and applied eighteen stitches there. Then she treated his left finger, which Gonzales had tried to bite off. Finally, she gave him a hepatitis shot and an antibiotic solution, just for good measure.

Meanwhile, Benjamin Gonzales was being treated for minor cuts and bruises back at the Santa Rita Jail infirmary. But instead of thanking the nurse, he kept yelling, "I want to see my lawyer!"

The wheels of justice may have been grinding along slowly as 1994 turned into 1995, but they were turning. Every day brought Benjamin Gonzales one step closer to a trial for the murder of Barbara Muszalski. By now he was thoroughly upset with his new lawyer, Les Chettle, who had replaced Howard Harplan after the Darrell Oliver attack. Gonzales petitioned the judge in the case, Judge Gordon Baranco, that he wanted to be his own counsel. He wrote, "I understand my rights and I'm willing and able to learn more from the law library."

But Judge Baranco was having none of this jail-house lawyer baloney. The request was denied.

Attorney Les Chettle knew that he was going to have his hands full with his client Benjamin Gonzales. But he had just come off a difficult murder case in nearby Union City, with positive results. In that trial his eleven-year-old client had been accused of stabbing to death forty-one-year-old Thomas Weinhofer as the man waited in his car in the parking lot of Union City High School. Several boys had been horsing around in the parking lot when they began rocking Weinhofer's car as he waited for his wife. Weinhofer got out and swore at them, and the boys began pummeling him with their fists. He swung back, and one of the boys pulled out a knife and stabbed him in the chest.

Weinhofer managed to get back in his car, and drive a block before collapsing. But before dying, he told several onlookers that some youths had attacked him.

Les Chettle's client became the focus of the police investigation because of his troubled past. He had been expelled from school the previous spring for savagely beating a classmate.

But through diligent work and research, Attorney Les Chettle was able to prove that his client had only been riding his bike in the area when the parking lot fracas broke out. Several independent witnesses attested to that. A new police investigation singled out the real killer, fourteen-year-old Tavo Collazo. Once Collazo confessed to the crime, Les Chettle's eleven-year-old client walked out of court, free as a bird.

Chettle hoped for a similar happy ending in the Benjamin Pedro Gonzales case. He already knew that a lot of the prosecution's case depended on circumstantial evidence. His biggest problem wasn't going to be that aspect. It was going to be Benjamin Gonzales himself.

On the same day that Gonzales was denied the right to represent himself, the new prosecutor in the case, Deputy D.A. Terry Wiley, appealed to the judge as his predecessor had done, requesting that Gonzales be shackled while in the courtroom. He wrote, "I request the defendant to be shackled to his chair at the table at all times the court is in session. These actions are necessary because the defendant is HIV positive and he had exhibited a propensity for violence, whose form includes biting and scratching. Thus, the defendant poses a deadly threat to court personnel and the jury, since the attorneys, clerks and jurors must walk past the defendant daily. If he is not shackled and decides to attack any of the above mentioned people, given his condition, could result in deadly and dire consequences for the person so attacked, if that person were to contract the AIDS virus."

Once again the request was denied. But within a week, the judge probably wished he had listened to the prosecutor's warning. Deputy D.A. Wiley's premonition about Benjamin Gonzales's propensity for violence would become all too real. It would make his attack on inmate Darrell Oliver look like a playground scuffle at an elementary schoolyard by comparison.

Nine

"An Absolute Bloody Mess"

Benjamin Gonzales may not have been looking forward to his trial, but one person was—Barbara Muszalski's daughter, Jamie. She told a *Tri-Valley Herald* reporter, "I just want to see justice done and so do all our friends. The whole family wants to get it over with because you can't close this until the trial is over. We've all been trying to get on with our lives and then [the trial] happens, which brings it all up once again."

A lot of people not looking forward to the trial were the prospective jurors. They could readily see that Benjamin Gonzales was already causing trouble in the courtroom, even in the jury selection phase, and a long and disruptive trial was sure to ensue. Many of the eighty prospective jurors requested to be dismissed because of financial reasons.

Gonzales was acting up at the Santa Rita

County Jail as well. On March 15, 1995, Deputy Caroll wrote in his report, "The above named inmate [Gonzales] has a court appearance scheduled for this date that requires him to be attired in civilian clothing. He has refused to change into civilian clothing."

Once he was actually in the courtroom, Gonzales's behavior got even worse. Angered by the fact that he did not want his new court-appointed defense counsel, Les Chettle, he argued with the judge and bailiffs at inappropriate times. He was always arguing with Chettle about a cockeyed scheme to have him extradited to South America so he could serve out his time there. He said he could have a girlfriend or even get married in a South American prison. He told Chettle he had contacts in the Colombian cartel who could help him do this. Once he was there, he said, he could bribe the jailers and get out of prison.

Chettle wouldn't even listen to this nonsense. In response, Gonzales went into a blinding rage and spat on his defense attorney. In sheer desperation, Judge Gordon Baranco cleared the courtroom.

Gonzales's temperament the next day was no better. Once again he refused to wear civilian clothing and constantly disrupted the courtroom proceedings. But he was saving the real fireworks for Friday, March 17, 1995. In defense counsel Les Chettle's own words, "After lunch [on March 17] I went into the holding cell in Department 8 to discuss the morning jury situation with Mr. Gonzales. He was seated in the stairwell and we had a discussion at that time. The bailiff left the door six inches ajar. My conversation with Gonzales centered around the morning jury selection and the four prepratory challenges that I exercised that morning. The conversation lasted three to four minutes. [At that time] he told me he wanted to tell me something, privately, and asked me would I close the door, which was behind me at the time. I turned and closed the door, and as I turned back I was struck. I was struck in the face several times, and one of the blows knocked my reading glasses off.

"Then I noticed he had something in his hand. It was a pencil. It looked to be three or four inches long. He was swinging at my chest area, and I jumped back, but I was struck in the left chest area. It punctured my skin. Then I was hit with the pencil behind my right ear. I had a three-quarter-inch cut on my upper lip as well. I bled through my shirt and from behind my right ear. I yelled for help."

Luckily for Attorney Chettle the door had not completely closed. Even more luckily, Deputy Les Moore, who was usually assigned to Judge Stanley Golde's courtroom next door, had been added as security to Judge Baranco's courtroom because of Gonzales's violent reputation. He heard Chettle's yelling in the stairwell, and within thirty seconds from the initiation of the attack, burst through the doorway, followed soon after by Deputy Eric Gulseth. What greeted their eyes was an incredible sight. In Gulseth's own words, "The defendant,

Benjamin Gonzales, was running up the stairwell and his attorney, Les Chettle, was sitting
on the ground and had blood running down
his face."

Gonzales was fast in his escape attempt, but
Deputy Moore was even faster. He tackled him
on the stairs, while Deputy Gulseth whipped
out a pair of handcuffs and cuffed Gonzales.
Then both of them held him down while he
wildly thrashed around on the stairs and
cursed them.

Deputy D.A. Terry Wiley entered the stairwell and beheld a scene he had never witnessed before in a courthouse. "I helped Les,
who was sprawled on the ground. When he
walked back into the courtroom, blood started
gushing out of the wound and paramedics
were called. He was an absolute bloody mess!
Deputy Les Moore probably saved Mr. Chettle's
life, given the violent nature of the attack."

Deputy D.A. Wiley couldn't resist getting in
a jab at Judge Baranco's decision not to
shackle Gonzales. He told a *Valley Times* reporter, "I told them this guy was going to attack someone. Based on my observations of
him in his few courtroom appearances, he had
a very volatile personality. And he had nothing
to lose by attacking someone. He knows there
is a fairly decent [murder] case against him."

Wiley noted, "This was the most vicious attack I've ever seen. I'm afraid this will force a
mistrial. The attack creates a natural conflict
between the defendant and his attorney."

Finally he gave praise once again to Deputy

Les Moore. "He responded in a lightning quick manner and was the one person Gonzales was frightened of."

Officer Moore downplayed his heroics by saying, "I just did my job." But he commented on the courtroom's security measures. "It's not set up to deal with the inmate of today," he said.

By his own crazy brand of judicial theatrics, Benjamin Gonzales made the whole Alameda County Court system stand up and take notice about its security apparatus. Sheriff's Commander Donna Green said, "This incident should remind the county that security of the courthouse ought to be a top priority. We're dealing with very dangerous people on a daily basis and we need not lose sight of that."

Superior Court Executive Officer Ron Overholt promised $50,000 in improvements in new weapons screening devices in the main courthouse in the next few weeks. He said, "We can't move on all locations, but certainly the main courthouse is a priority."

Defense attorney Les Chettle was admitted to Highland Hospital for treatment, just like Gonzales's previous jail-house victim, Darrell Oliver. It didn't take Chettle long to drop from being Gonzales's attorney, and filing charges against him. Now on top of a murder charge, Gonzales had an assault with a deadly weapon charge as well.

But despite the new charge, Benjamin Gonzales could feel pretty satisfied with himself. The attack had indeed caused a mistrial, just as Deputy D.A. Terry Wiley had predicted. And it did one more important thing. Gonzales was scheduled for a competency hearing whether he should stand trial for murder at all. It would mean the difference between being sent to prison for twenty-five years to life, and being sent to the more easygoing confines of a mental institution.

Victim Barbara Muszalski, 49.
(Photo courtesy Alameda County Superior Court)

While searching for the missing Muszalski, investigators found bloodstains on the driveway of neighbor Dave Williams's ranch.

Three days after she disappeared, Muszalski's Chevy pickup was found in an airport garage.
(Photo courtesy Alameda County Superior Court)

The soles of Muszalski's tennis shoe-clad feet
were visible in the hay in her pickup.
(Photo courtesy Alameda County Superior Court)

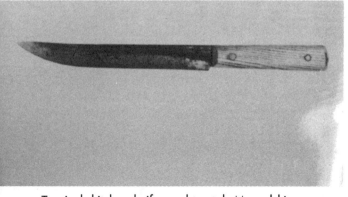

Ten-inch kitchen knife used to stab Muszalski
was found in the pickup's cab.
(Photo courtesy Alameda County Superior Court)

Gonzales jailed in county

Suspect in rancher's death is returned after yearlong search

BENJAMIN GONZALES

Muszalski's murderer *(center)* was caught after a year-long nationwide search. *(Photo courtesy* Contra Costa Newspapers*)*

Benjamin Pedro Gonzales used at least twelve aliases.
(Photo courtesy Alameda County Superior Court)

Previously convicted of prostitution and disorderly conduct, Gonzales, 25, was convicted of assault with a deadly weapon in 1984.
(Photo courtesy Alameda County Superior Court)

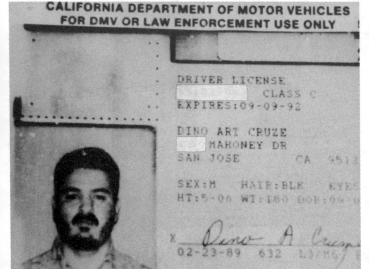

Gonzales's 1989 California driver's license gave his name as Dino Art Cruze. *(Photo courtesy Alameda County Superior Court)*

Victim Dondi Johnson, 22.
(Photo courtesy Alameda County Superior Court)

Johnson's burned-out 1977 Pontiac Trans Am.
(Photo courtesy Alameda County Superior Court)

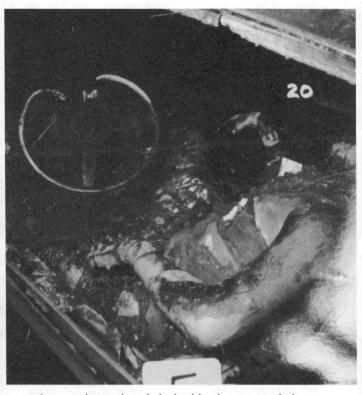

Johnson's burned and slashed body was inside her car.
(Photo courtesy Alameda County Superior Court)

Victim Yvonne Hausley, 22.
(Photo courtesy Alameda County Superior Court)

Show World Theater in Manhattan where Hausley worked.
(Photo courtesy Alameda County Superior Court)

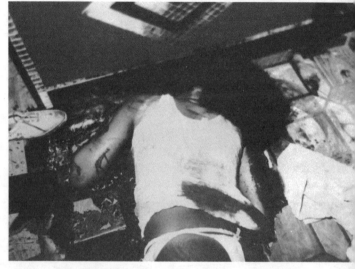
Hausley's body was found in a pool of blood.
(Photo courtesy Alameda County Superior Court)

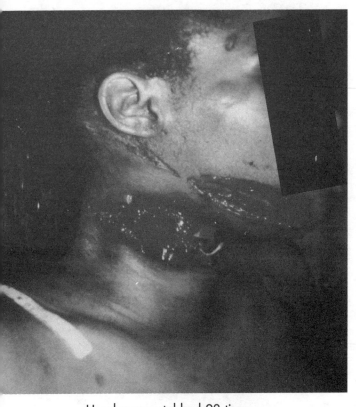
Hausley was stabbed 28 times.
(Photo courtesy Alameda County Superior Court)

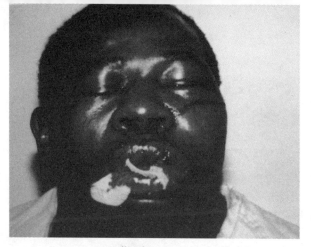

Inmate Darrell Oliver was attacked by
Gonzales on April 15, 1994.
(Photo courtesy Alameda County Superior Court)

Bloody shower where Gonzales attacked Oliver.
(Photo courtesy Alameda County Superior Court)

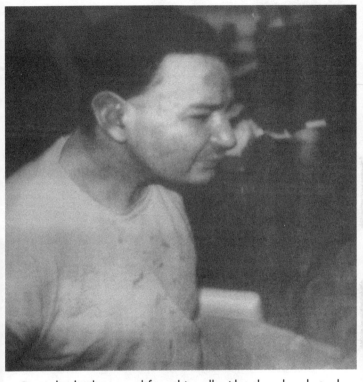
Gonzales had escaped from his cell with a handmade tool.
(Photo courtesy Alameda County Superior Court)

Defense Attorney Les Chettle was attacked by Gonzales in the courthouse on March 17, 1995. *(Photos courtesy Alameda County Superior Court)*

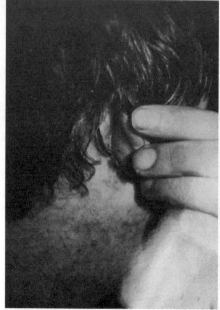

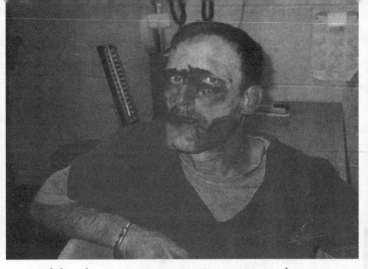

While riding in a prison van, Francis MacArthur was attacked by a handcuffed Gonzales on November 5, 1998. *(Photo courtesy Alameda County Superior Court)*

Lieutenant Dale Toussaint. *(Photo courtesy Dale Toussaint)*

LAPD Detective
Frank Bolan.
*(Photo courtesy
Frank Bolan)*

Inspector
Brian Lerche.
*(Photo courtesy
Brian Lerche)*

III

THE GONZALES SHUFFLE

Ten

Crazy Like a Fox

In September 1995, Benjamin Gonzales was evaluated separately by court-appointed psychiatrists Dr. Larry Wornian and Dr. Karen Gudiksen. They still carried the archaic title of "alienist" in the court system. After several hours of speaking with Gonzales and administering various tests, Dr. Gudiksen came to the conclusion that Gonzales was most likely suffering from AIDS dementia. She also intimated that there was the possibility of some schizophrenia and that he was not competent to stand trial. Dr. Wornian's conclusion was also that Gonzales was not competent to stand trial. They surmised Gonzales could not aid in his defense or give helpful information to his lawyer because of his incompetency.

With these reports in hand, Judge Gordon Baranco wrote on October 27, 1995, "Mr Gonzales's mental condition is such that he will need a period of hospitalization in order for him to be restored to competency. Due to the nature of charges against him, he will need to be treated in a secure and structured institution. It is ordered that the sheriff of Alameda County deliver the defendant to said Atascadero State Hospital."

Atascadero is a small city of 25,000 people located on California's beautiful central coast not far from San Luis Obispo. Just over the hill, publishing magnate William Randolph Hearst built his dream home—Hearst Castle. With its 115 rooms sitting atop La Cuesta Encantada—the Enchanted Hill—overlooking the blue Pacific at San Simeon, the main house did indeed look like a fantastic Moorish castle in its palatial setting. Amid pools, gardens and statuary, the castle evoked a bygone era of grace and immense wealth.

Atascadero State Hospital may not have been a Hearst Castle, but it didn't look bad, especially from afar. Situated on rolling, oak-studded hills under the warm central coast sun, the grounds looked more like a park than a mental institution. Someone viewing it from a distance might confuse it for a resort.

But behind the rolling hills and green lawns was a world away from the "real world." All of Atascadero's more than 1,000 patients had some kind of criminal background, and more than 250 of them were sex offenders. Some were mentally ill, but others were just killing time—watching television, hanging around in the arts and crafts room, awaiting trial. Many, like Benjamin Gonzales, were deemed not competent to stand trial. But if Atascadero had its way, that would change.

There were varying programs designed to restore the inmates to mental competency, and some of the inmates were severely disturbed with ailments such as schizophrenia or bipolar disorder. They were a prime group for Benjamin Gonzales to observe and emulate.

There were the sexual predators who were not mentally ill, but had been dumped there by the state of California because no one knew where else to put them. The rapists and child molesters who walked around in standard-issue khaki clothes were a grave danger to other patients. Gonzales also kept tabs on these. From his Hollywood prostitution days, Gonzales knew all about sexual deviancy. He was no novice when it came to knowing all their tricks. But he was also keeping his eyes and ears open. For him, Atascadero was a school in how to act crazy. As long as he appeared to be incompetent, he wasn't going anywhere and that was just fine with him.

Carla Jacobs, a board member of the Alliance for the Mentally Ill, told Jim Rendon, a journalist for the *San Jose Metro News,* about these sexual predators in state hospitals such as Atascadero. She said, "I have no problem with keeping sex offenders off the street. I do have a problem when the state confuses them with people that have a mental illness." Dumping the predators in with the general population of a mental illness institution caused real problems.

Forensic psychiatrist Jules Burstein agreed. He told Jim Rendon, "There is no mental disorder that is related to rape. It's like trying to find a mental disorder for a guy that holds up liquor stores. As soon as sex is involved, we say he must be sick. There are a lot of crimes you have to be crazy to commit, but we don't institutionalize those people."

Even the man who ran the sexually violent predator program at Atascadero agreed that these criminals walking his halls were different from the general population there. Craig Nelson told the reporter, "They have a psychological disorder. They have sexual desires that most of society condemns. Something has gone wrong."

Benjamin Gonzales fell into the periphery of this group. He wasn't the classic sexual predator. He never raped or sexually molested his victims. But his murders of women were almost orgasmic in their fury. The stabbings were so violent and brutal that they created some kind of release in Gonzales akin to a climax in sex. He had one more thing in common with this group—he wasn't insane, though he was doing his best to mask that fact now. One thing he learned very quickly at Atascadero—it was a whole lot better here than awaiting trial for murder in Alameda County's Santa Rita Jail.

The sexually violent predators he observed posed a huge problem for the mental hospital. Many were advised by their attorneys not to participate in the treatment programs. Some sabotaged group sessions. According to Jim Rendon, one man even complained that nurses were not good looking enough to change his sexual focus. Fighting between the non-mentally ill patients was chronic.

All sorts of programs swirled around Benjamin Gonzales in his stay at Atascadero. The chief one for patients in his category was focused on self-examination. Inmates were told to write accounts of their crimes and try to determine what led them to victimize and what clues to look for in their behavior that would likely lead to rape or molesting. Gonzales short-circuited this right away, because he claimed not to know how to read and write.

Writer Jim Rendon was allowed a peek into these sessions. He wrote, "In a small room reserved for substance abuse classes, two hospital patients sit behind a wooden table. Their psychiatrist, Gabrielle Palladino, has refused to tell me their names or even their county, citing privacy concerns. Yet in a strange paradox, every word these men utter in the most private therapy session can be used against them in court.

"Both men wear the khaki shirts and pants that all inmates are issued in the hospital. The man sitting closest to me blushes when he talks. Though his large hands are steady, his nose quivers slightly, betraying his nerves.

" 'I realized I have been a screw-up most of my life,' he says in a surprisingly quiet voice. 'Every time I was busted and went to jail, I said I would change. I was just kidding myself. Atas-

cadero has helped me in a way prison never
could.'

"In group therapy he discovered the things
he has in common with other offenders. 'A lot
of us had abusive parents, we used drugs and
alcohol, we were sexually abused as kids.' He
pauses for a moment. 'It's not an excuse,' he
says. 'People have been through that and not
offended. What makes us different?' he asks
rhetorically. Indeed, it's a question no one can
answer.

"Next to him is a smaller man with a beard
and glasses. He is a fast talker with a rare kind
of charisma. He is the kind of guy you want
to go have a beer with just to hear him spin
a tale. He is a convicted child molester.

" 'Before my offense I knew I was going
downhill,' he says. 'But there was no place to
go. I was married with three kids. If you're a
drug user or a gambler, there are programs. If
you are a sex abuser, you just can't walk in off
the street.'

"Both men spent years in prison before they
got here, and neither man got treatment there.
Of Palladino's one hundred patients, only one
said he enrolled in a treatment plan in prison.
'There are three things that can get you killed
in prison,' says Palladino, a former prison psychiatrist. 'Owing money, snitching and being a
sex offender. Just getting these men to admit
their crimes is a huge accomplishment.' "

Benjamin Gonzales may have watched the
others tell about their crimes, but he certainly
wasn't talking about his. Not to the other in-

mates of Atascadero and certainly not to the psychiatrists. He wasn't admitting anything, especially when his words could become part of the court record and be used against him. He kept his mouth shut and his eyes wide open. Of particular interest were the truly mentally ill. He noticed how they walked, how they talked and what they said in response to questions. He stored all the knowledge away for future use.

Benjamin Gonzales adapted to his new surroundings better than the doctors might have supposed. Not in the sense of getting "better" to stand trial. Rather, it was just the opposite. He was doing everything possible not to return to Alameda County. He may not have been formally educated, but he was no dummy. He had well-developed street smarts and he knew that if he ever appeared rational, it would be a quick trip back to Oakland to stand trial for the murder of Barbara Muszalski and the assault on defense attorney Les Chettle. He was already a master at being a chameleon, changing into multiple personalities and identities. And there was no doubt that he was already borderline in a lot of ways as far as mental health went. All he had to do was amplify his already strange behavior.

But the psychiatrists at Atascadero were no dummies either. Staff psychiatrist Mark Germaine, M.D., observed Benjamin Gonzales well, and he noted how Gonzales interacted with other patients and staff members. He could not yet judge if Gonzales was faking symptoms of mental illness, but he believed that he was not as incompetent as he sometimes let on. Certainly not so incompetent that he couldn't understand court proceedings.

Dr. Germaine wrote on June 4, 1996, "The interdisciplinary treatment team met with Mr. Gonzales to evaluate his mental competence to stand trial. He is clear and focused and answered court-related questions easily. Mr. Gonzales demonstrated an understanding of court procedures, the roles and functions of courtroom officials, and the available pleas he could enter in court. He also demonstrates an understanding of the charges against him and the possible consequences of each plea. Mr. Gonzales verbalized a willingness to cooperate with his attorney in a rational manner in the preparation of his defense."

With this report in hand, the director of the facility wrote, "This defendant has been under treatment and observation since the date of admission to the hospital. It is the consensus of the clinical staff and the medical director of the hospital that the defendant is now able to understand the nature of the charges against the defendant and can cooperate with the attorney in subject's defense. A speedy trial is important for maintenance of trial competency."

Within days, Benjamin Gonzales found himself on a prison bus motoring up Highway 101 to stand trial in Alameda County. But it did not turn out to be a one-way trip by any means. Gonzales had learned his little "mental illness" secrets well from observing other patients, and he was about to give a bravura performance before the court-appointed psychiatrists in Alameda County.

Dr. Wornian went to visit Gonzales at the Santa Rita Jail, and Gonzales complained to the doctor, "They didn't give me time to wake up here. I couldn't sleep because of my stomach last night. I don't like AZT. It upsets my stomach. My T-cell count is forty-three, so I don't need AZT."

When asked by Dr. Wornian to repeat the alphabet, Gonzales said, "I haven't sung that song in a long time. I don't know. I need something smaller [to recite]."

Asked specifically about his new court-appointed lawyer, Albert Thews, Gonzales said, "My attorney, he's gonna come and talk to me, and, and . . . he's gonna come talk to me. I don't like your machine [pointing at Dr. Wornian's notebook computer]. It's like you have a toy, and I don't have nothin'. [Then back to his attorney.] He's gonna come in and help with my forty-three T cells in my stomach."

Dr. Wornian noted Gonzales's erratic behavior, and the inability to perform even simple tasks, like repeating the alphabet, and concluded, "Mr. Gonzales is not competent to stand trial."

The Alameda Court also appointed Dr. Joel Fort to appraise Gonzales's competency. Dr. Fort noticed that Gonzales had lost twenty-five pounds since he had been down in Atascadero, and that he was not taking his AZT medication to combat AIDS. He wrote, "It is puzzling that he [Gonzales] was found competent by the staff of Patton [one of the hospitals affiliated with Atascadero State Hospital], but unfortunately, he is presently incompetent as he was last September. Thus, I conclude he has not regained his mental competency."

With such reports in hand, the judge didn't have much choice but to send Gonzales back to Atascadero State Hospital. The report read, "Pursuant to Section 1370 of the Penal Code, it is recommended that Benjamin Pedro Gonzales be committed to Atascadero State Hospital."

Round one to Gonzales. But the fight over his mental capacity was far from over.

Once back in Atascadero, Gonzales didn't have long to stay there. He was shipped off to Patton State Hospital in southern California near San Bernadino. It was not too far down the freeway from where Dondi Johnson had been murdered.

Patton State for the criminally insane sat behind barbed-wire fences in a semi-arid setting. The San Gabriel Mountains loomed above it like a dark cloud that would not pass away. Behind its walls, it had programs similar to Atascadero, and one more that was truly unique. It was a drama workshop for mentally ill patients sponsored by the Imagination Workshop. This had been created in 1969 by Margaret Ladd, of *Falcon Crest* fame, as a way for mentally ill patients to focus their feelings. In the years since, such actors as Susan Sarandon, Blythe Danner, Sam Waterston, Cher and Henry Winkler had been part of drama workshops behind Patton's walls. There were also many relatively unknown actors who would take time off from movies and television to be part of the groups. As one told journalist Joy Horowitz, "You have to put back. Not to sound Goody Two Shoes, but that's the reason. You see results. You have to find the time in your life to do these kinds of things, because being obsessed with work, work, work—it's not going to happen. At the same time it helps your work . . . it's about acting as a form of healing opposed to the Hollywood way."

Horowitz wrote, "The Imagination Workshop stayed away from psychodrama. The participants never played themselves, and the workshops didn't focus on pathology. The focus was on the enjoyment of creating. And sometimes the mask of madness is stripped away, if just for a moment."

The performances themselves varied wildly. In one set, the participants pretended to be singers such as Dolly Parton and Michael Jackson. They even created their own song, "When You Lend a Hand, You Get One Back." As one actor told Joy Horowitz, "It's pretty hokey, a sort of 'Psychotics Amateur Hour.' Each patient takes a turn at the microphone, sometimes barely audible, singing an original tune with a goofy hat on and, often, a dull expression. But virtually every performer clearly craves the very thing he or she usually fears

most: human contact. Their involvement
makes them forget their disability and reach,
albeit only momentarily, across the barrier between them and us. And given the progress of
the revue in the span of a month—from a rag-
tag jumble of psychotic rants to well-rehearsed
expression of human desire—their efforts seem
nothing short of heroic."

There's no record of Benjamin Gonzales
ever participating in the Imagination Workshop. But he knew real psychosis when he saw
it and heard it. While he didn't interact much
with other patients and staff, he kept his eyes
and ears wide open, and he took in everything
around him.

Conditions at Patton State Hospital were not
all Imagination dramas and self-help groups.
Not unlike prison, it was also a dangerous
place. Case in point is what happened to a patient designated only as K.C. He was a twenty-
year-old patient diagnosed with schizophrenia,
a history of substance abuse, a seizure disorder
and Klinefelter's syndrome (a condition in
which a male has an additional X chromo-
some). During his stay at Patton, he received
medication that included Prolixin Deconoate,
Cogentin Tegretol, Dilantin and Imipramine.

According to a report by the Protection and
Advocacy Corporation, they followed doctor's
orders by placing the patient on a suicide watch
after he had tried to commit suicide. The watch
was to include a staff member checking on the
patient every fifteen minutes. It was noticed that
the patient was agitated and seemed to have dif-

ficulty breathing. He was also hallucinating that mosquitoes were in his bed.

After refusing to take Prolixin (a neurological drug), K.C. was injected with the neuroleptic Haldol. Hospital reports show that the patient then went into the bathroom at three A.M. At six A.M., he was found in full cardiac arrest, prone on his bed, by a psychiatric technician. The body was in full rigor mortis. As this generally takes several hours to occur, the PAC's expert concluded that the patient had died shortly after the injection.

Benjamin Gonzales was walking through a virtual minefield at Patton State Hospital. If the administration of drugs didn't get him, there was always the potential of sudden and explosive violence. According to the *San Bernardino County Sun*, several Patton psych technicians were injured in a melee when two patients ambushed them in the hallway as they escorted another patient to an isolation area. Other staff members rushed to their aid, and by the time the fight was over, the techs and nurses had suffered broken wrists, numerous sprains and cuts, bumps and bruises. Of the ten employees involved, six were injured severely enough to be sent home or to local hospitals.

The *San Bernardino County Sun* reported, "The three patients involved in the attack were all criminal defendants who were committed to Patton after being found incompetent to stand trial. Hospital officials are investigating what appears to be an organized attack. Such coordinated attacks are more commonly associated with sane prison inmates than patients in mental hospitals. Patton officials are evaluating the three patients to determine if they are truly mentally incompetent. Increasingly, defendants are pretending to be deranged, since the adoption of the state's three-strikes law. The growing number of assaults by such patients poses serious safety problems for hospital staff. . . . A 1996 Patton study found that 10 percent of the patients committed to the 1,225 bed hospital were faking insanity."

Obviously Benjamin Gonzales had company in his deception of mental incompetency. The doctors at Patton had their faculties on alert however, and as time went on, it appeared more and more that Gonzales was malingering. They had one great advantage over the Alameda court-appointed psychiatrists—they could observe him day in and day out, not just an hour during some interview. They noticed that Benjamin Gonzales was not consistent in his supposed mental deficiencies. He could at times be very rational. As the months passed, the conclusion became more and more evident—Gonzales was faking it.

Acting superintendant and medical director of Patton State Hospital, James Rosenthal, wrote the judge up in Oakland, "I recommend Benjamin Gonzales be sent back for a speedy trial."

Like a human ping-pong ball, Gonzales boarded the bus for a trip back to his old surroundings at the Santa Rita Jail in Alameda

County. But the court-appointed psychiatrists were not yet through with him. If anything, their sessions became more wide-ranging and intense. With all the knowledge Benjamin Gonzales had stored away about mentally ill people, he was ready for them.

During his interviews with Dr. Larry Wornian, Gonzales was kept shackled (except for short neuropsychological screenings). Gonzales was easily distracted, and throughout Wornian's examinations he whined about his aches and pains, his low T-cell count, his having less than a year to live because he had AIDS, and he repeatedly requested crackers for his nausea.

Wornian administered a short mental status examination. Although Gonzales knew his date of birth, he was unsure of his age and dismissed the offer of paper and pencil to work it out by saying he was not good at math. He did not know the current year and was unable to name all of the months or even correctly recite the alphabet (he repeated some letters and omitted others).

As part of the examination, Gonzales was asked if he knew the charges against him. He replied, "I use drugs. I'm not goin' to do anything to anybody." He was also unable to explain the role of a prosecutor. Given this apparent limited understanding of his circumstances, Wornian had Gonzales undergo several neuropsychological tests. These included clock drawing, the Bender-Gestalt, and the Neurobehavioral Mental Status Examination.

Throughout the testing Gonzales complained, "It's like school. I don't like school. Why are you doing this to me?"

Dr. Wornian reported that, "There were a number of tasks that strongly recommended an originally based dementing process. One additional element seen in this administration that was not seen previously, as a pronounced tendency toward preservation—that is, repeating oneself on the Bender-Gestalt test, Mr. Gonzales substituted impulsively drawn loops, but the left-most portion of the semi-circle continues in a straight line—literally he could not stop himself.

In Dr. Wornian's written opinion, "There were a range of features found in Mr. Gonzales's performance that are pathogenic—that is, his efforts display a number of symptoms that are taken to characteristics of a disease process, and not simply the results of his efforts to be evasive or uncooperative. . . . There were simply too many features of his overall presentation that recommend the presence of an established dementia. . . . There are emotional disturbances that are seen, ranging from agitation, to depression, to both delusions and paranoid thought processes have been seen and unless Mr. Gonzales has undertaken an effort to school himself in such fields as behavioral neurology, it seems highly unlikely that such actions could have been faked. Could he have observed behaviors of other patients at Patton [Hospital]? While this cannot be ruled out with certainty, the reports from Patton recommend that he was fairly withdrawn and socially isolated so this prospect does not seem likely."

Dr. Wornian's conclusion to the judge was that, unfortunately, the window in which there was some degree of clarity on Gonzales's part seems to have closed once again. As such, I believe that the evidence warrants that Mr. Gonzales remains incompetent."

Dr. Wornian had psychiatrist Dr. Karen Gudiksen's independent report to back him up. She stated she was not sure whether or not Gonzales recognized her from previous interviews. She noted that he made his usual complaints about his stomach and expressed suspicions regarding his treatment by custodial staff at the Santa Rita Jail. Gonzales's response to Gudiksen's questions were that he thought that the interview was taking place in Patton State Hospital, he did not remember that he had been in Atascadero State Hospital, did not know the date, claimed he did not know his next court date or the name of his attorney, but did know his own name. Gudiksen stated, "[Gonzales's] memory, both for the nearly immediate recall and for remote items, was impaired. He did admit that he was a drug addict, but seemed to think his charges were related to substance abuse rather than the much more serious charges of murder and assault. He seemed to lose train of thought during our interview. There was a child-like quality to much of our interview. He demonstrated lability and cried during the interview."

Gudiksen's opinion was that Gonzales had AIDS dementia. She stated, "While he may have been restored to mental competency while a patient at Patton State Hospital, it is my opinion at this time that Benjamin P. Gonzales is once again at the present time a mentally incompetent person. He is unable to cooperate with defense counsel in preparation and presentation of a rational defense."

With such recommendations by the experts, the judge had no choice but to return Gonzales to Patton State Hospital. Round two to Gonzales. Wags at the Alameda County Courthouse began referring to the process as "The Gonzales Shuffle."

In one respect, Benjamin Gonzales was not getting any better and it was no scam. If he wasn't incompetent and unable to help his attorney, some would indeed think he was at least crazy for what he did next. For, right in the middle of a state hospital where he was being held in lieu of trial for murdering a woman he had stalked, he began stalking another woman who was a nurse at Patton! It absolutely highlighted the fact that if he wasn't insane in a legal sense, he was at least pressing the borders of rational behavior.

There would be from this point on three women who came down in the records as having a profound impact on Benjamin Gonzales's life. Two of them would be known by their first names only—Cindy and Carole. The third of these, Sandi Nakamura, would have the most important impact of all. It was toward her that all his obsession and stalking was now directed.

Sandi Nakamura was Gonzales's primary nurse and AIDS counselor at Patton State Hospital. She was ten years his senior, and even though she was "Anglo" as he put it, she was married to a Japanese man. Their age difference bothered Gonzales not at all. It hadn't bothered him with Barbara Muszalski and it didn't with Sandi. She was kind to him and listened to him and that was all that mattered. She listened to all his tales of being abused as a child and his run-ins with the law. Because she had a caring nature, he began to obsess about her, as he had done with the others. He mistook her kindness to be a mutual bond of affection. He began to fantasize about their relationship. Before long, "Nurse Sandi" was no longer just his nurse; she became in his mind his lover.

Gonzales fantasized about them having sex in the conference rooms, in the hallways, even in the linen closets. After a while his fantasies grew to such lengths that he believed that they actually did have sex. The line between reality and fantasy became completely blurred in his mind.

And just like with the other women, he could act gentle and meek when he wanted to. He brought out the maternal instinct in Sandi as he had done in Barbara Muszalski. He seemed like someone who needed caring and attention. Nurse Sandi not only listened to him, but took care of his AIDS-related problems. Because she knew all the problems associated with AIDS patients, she may have attributed his mood swings to his medication and environment. After all, it would have been a remarkable person not to be affected by all that was going on around him in Patton State Hospital, where there were some truly mentally ill people. But Gonzales's illness was of a more specific nature, and Nurse Sandi had no way of knowing what violence lay just beneath that gentle surface.

Benjamin Gonzales could not give a damn about the therapy sessions, or Imagination Workshops, or any of the other programs that supposedly would make him get better. But the one thing he did care about being in Patton was Sandi Nakamura. What could be a better set-up? Here he was avoiding trial and had the new woman of his dreams working within its confines. He didn't even have to go to some clinic to see her. She came to see him.

Before long Gonzales would recount, "She knew me better than anyone. She knew all the information. Sandi knows the different aspects of me. She knows the different people inside my head . . . which are spirits."

He wasn't telling her all his fantasies yet—not by a long shot. But his fantasies were running riot by now. He convinced himself that she would leave her husband for him—just as Barbara Muszalski was supposed to do. Sandi would help him get out of Patton. She would go so far as to buy a gun to help him escape. They were going to buy rings together. They were going to be married. He'd leave all this insanity behind and live happily ever after with Nurse Sandi.

While all these incredible fantasies were raging in Gonzales's mind, one psychiatrist in the Bay Area did not believe he was incompetent to stand trial. Gonzales may have been "crazy" in some regards, but he was not so insane as to be unable to understand court proceedings or help his lawyer in his own defense. The one psychiatrist who thought Gonzales was faking it was Dr. Jules Burstein—the same Dr. Burstein whom the writer Jim Rendon had interviewed.

Dr. Burstein had a background in evaluating mental competency. From 1977 to 1981, he was the senior staff psychologist at the Alameda County Criminal Justice Clinic, which served inmates at the Santa Rita Jail. During that time he examined 2,500 inmates, both men and women, to determine if they suffered from mental illness. Some obviously did, and were determined to be able to present a psychiatric defense.

From 1981 on, Dr. Burstein had his own private practice, but he was still called upon numerous times by both defense lawyers and deputy district attorneys to determine if an alleged criminal was mentally ill and too incompetent to stand trial. In this capacity, and because of his reputation in the field, he was on the Superior Court panel of psychologists in four Bay Area counties. Since 1981, he had examined nearly 700 defendants for mental capacity issues.

As to the term "malingering," of which Benjamin Gonzales had been accused at Patton State Hospital, Dr. Burstein had his own definition. He said, "It's the faking of symptoms which are feigned to mitigate one's level of criminal responsibility. That is, a desire to be seen as sick or disturbed rather than bad or evil. In the criminal justice system, defendants have an obvious inspiration for lying because it may be helpful to the ultimate judicial decision in their case. I get to see a lot of liars and fakers and people who exaggerate symptoms."

In 1997, Dr. Burstein was appointed by the court to examine Benjamin Gonzales at the Santa Rita Jail. As soon as Gonzales took one look at Dr. Burstein, he must have sensed that this man was going to be different from the rest of the court-appointed psychologists he had seen. Gonzales had cooperated with doctors Gudiksen, Fort and Wornian on several occasions, but he was having none of it with Dr. Burstein. He absolutely refused to talk to him.

Dr. Burstein spent fifteen minutes trying to get Gonzales to recite the alphabet. Gonzales refused. As Dr. Burstein said later, "That was the first time in over twenty years of practice I have had an inmate refuse to recite the alphabet."

Dr. Burstein asked Gonzales to sign a release so that he could look at his Patton State Hospital records. Gonzales refused, saying that this would lead to having his head x-rayed.

Dr. Burstein had never heard this excuse before, so he had the clerk at the jail clinic come in and tell Gonzales that this would not happen. Gonzales still refused.

Realizing that he wasn't going to get anywhere with Benjamin Gonzales, Dr. Burstein terminated the interview. It was already becoming apparent to him that he wasn't dealing with someone who was seriously mentally ill in the legal sense, but rather a person who was devious and trying to thwart all attempts to reveal his true competency to stand trial.

Dr. Burstein sought a court order to allow him to see the Patton State records. He didn't get a full accounting, but what he saw reinforced what he already suspected about Gonzales's malingering. He later said, "Despite his [Gonzales's] opposition to be formally interviewed by me, I had enough data to form an opinion, and that opinion was that he was competent to stand trial. There was nothing that I saw in Mr. Gonzales's demeanor, in his behavior, his language, his general mental status and presentation on the day that I saw him that suggested the presence of any major psychiatric disorder. Secondly, the records from Patton were extremely compelling. I made liberal reference to them on page three of my report, and there are many different concerns I have from these records indicating that staff there who saw Mr. Gonzales around the clock concluded that he was a malingerer, someone who clearly does not suffer any major mental disorder. Several clinicians made comments about there not being any indication of psychiatric symptoms or dementia. And finally, just before my opinion, I had a quote in which one of the clinicians stated, 'Mr. Gonzales's clinical presentation is consistent with the intentional production of false or grossly exaggerated symptoms of cognitive impairment, and the performance of someone who is not fully co-operative with attempts to evaluate his competency to stand trial.' "

Not that Dr. Burstein always came down on the side of the prosecutor. In an infamous trial in Santa Cruz County, he had stated in court that the defendant accused of a heinous crime was mentally incompetent. Seventeen-year-old Donald Schmidt was accused of raping and murdering three-year-old Marihia Silvola. While Marihia's mother, Leslie, was on a metham-phetimine high in her mountain cabin, Donald sodomized the young girl and held her head under water to stifle her screams.

But he had gone too far. Donald Schmidt had only meant to quiet her. Instead, he killed her.

Neighbor Gail Levey testified that she heard someone yelling, "Oh, my God! Oh, my God!"

She ran outside to investigate and found Donald Schmidt standing in the road, waving his arms and yelling. She grabbed Schmidt and told him to calm down. She said she was a nurse and could help if someone was hurt. When they both went into the cabin, Levey found the little girl lying on the floor. The mother, Leslie, was totally unconcerned. She swallowed some more pills, took a swig from a bottle of vodka and muttered, "This is just great! This is all I need!"

Once the case went to trial, the mother was in one courtroom, and Donald Schmidt in another. Prosecutor Mike Barton tried to portray Schmidt as plenty sophisticated and able to stand trial as an adult, which could bring a sentence of twenty-five years to life.

But defense witness Dr. Jules Burstein had another take on Donald Schmidt. He discovered that Donald Schmidt too had been a victim of abuse. His own parents had abused him as a child, and as a young teenager, he had lived with a man who constantly sodomized him. He concluded that Schmidt, even though he was seventeen, was emotionally the equivalent of a twelve-year-old.

Superior Court Judge Tom Black agreed, and ruled that Donald Schmidt would be tried as a juvenile, not an adult. The ruling meant that Schmidt would automatically be sentenced to the California Youth Authority, where he would serve no longer than until his twenty-seventh birthday.

But Benjamin Gonzales was another story. As far as Dr. Jules Burstein was concerned, Gonzales was putting on an act and pulling the wool over the other court-appointed psychiatrists' eyes.

Down in southern California at Patton, the medical director, Dr. Rosenthal, was just as adamant as Dr. Burstein about Gonzales, and he was not amused with the state of affairs. In fact,

he was beside himself. Every time he returned
Gonzales to Alameda County to stand trial, a
team of court-appointed psychiatrists overruled
his opinion and sent Gonzales right back. But
Dr. Rosenthal had his own team of experts,
and he had determined that this charade
should end, once and for all. Whether he set
an elaborate trap for Gonzales to fall into, or
whether he just got lucky the third time
around, only he knows for sure. But it was
something as simple as the date on a letter that
was to trip Benjamin Gonzales up for good.

Gonzales had constantly contended that the
present year was 1986, when in fact it was now
1997. Then one day in July 1997, a doctor at
Patton State Hospital asked Gonzales the number of the year, one more time. He immediately pronounced it to be 1986. But that very
day, a member of the hospital staff innocently
asked Gonzales to date an outgoing letter. Ben
not only put the correct day on the letter, he
wrote down the correct year as well.

Within hours a doctor's report was out about
his slipup. It read: "Without hesitation, Mr.
Gonzales put the correct date on the letter.
Clearly indicating that his disorientation for
the time during the interview was feigned."

Suddenly all his lying and duplicitous answers
at the interviews were called into question.
Worse was to follow for him soon thereafter. He
always claimed he could not write, but a letter
he had written to Nurse Sandi Nakamura at Pat-

ton was confiscated. It contained the words written by him—"manipulate," "destruction," "agony," and "frustration."

Even the Alameda County court-appointed psychiatrists had their eyes opened at this point. The answers to Dr. Wornian's own question, "Could he [Gonzales] have observed behaviors of other patients at Patton?" was obviously, "Yes." Gonzales may not have been a student of behavioral sciences, but he was a student of human behavior. He had carefully watched the truly mentally ill patients at Patton State Hospital and learned to mimic their behavior when it came time to be interviewed by court-appointed psychiatrists. By this means he was able to display classic textbook symptoms.

He was a keen observer of details and incredibly patient and inventive. The antisensor device he had constructed from a plain plastic comb at Santa Rita Jail already proved that. With nothing but time on his hands at Patton, he had watched and learned just what it took to fool even the experts.

It was not easy for the court-appointed psychiatrists to eat crow, but even they now recommended that Gonzales be returned to Alameda County to stand trial. Only Karen Gudiksen actually talked to *Contra Costa Times* reporter David Holbrook about how Gonzales had fooled her. She said, "They [Patton State Hospital] already have a diagnosis and any treatment the patient has undergone. That's outside information from people who already have contact with the patient. Without those

records, I and my peers are limited to basing
our opinions on Gonzales's sanity from face-to-
face evaluations that last an hour or less. Such
contacts make it easier for a patient to fool a
professional."

Dr. Jules Burstein, the Berkeley psychologist
who testified to Gonzales's sanity at the hearing, brought up one important fact that the
others had ignored. He told Holbrook, "There
were other sources doctors failed to tap that
could have offered insight into Gonzales's competence. While court-appointed doctors have
no right to a patient's records, they are allowed
to talk with other jail staff members, particularly sheriff's deputies."

Court records showed that the court-appointed doctors never talked to the jail staff or
deputies. Dr. Burstein admitted, "That's pretty
unheard of [talking to jail personnel], but all
you would have to do is ask the deputies who
see this guy day after day whether he's hearing
voices or says he doesn't know where he is. If
he's not, then you have to wonder why he's
doing it only when you're talking to him."

Benjamin Gonzales's days of avoiding trial
at Atascadero and Patton State hospitals were
over. The new judge in the case, number
three if anyone was counting, was the Honorable Jeffrey Horner, and he ordered that Gonzales would stand trial at Oakland's Superior
Court, to take place in August 1997. He was
determined that Gonzales would cause no dis-
ruptions in his courtroom. Unlike his predecessors, he was willing to entertain the more

stringent security measures that had been advised by the prosecution from the very beginning. But whether Judge Horner would be any more successful in this than his predecessors remained to be seen.

Eleven

The Stalker

Two men would now have a huge impact on the fate of Benjamin Pedro Gonzales. One was defense attorney Albert Thews, and the other, Alameda County Deputy District Attorney Morris Jacobson.

Albert Thews had the dubious honor of representing Gonzales by court appointment. Not too far in the back of his mind had to be the mental image of what had happened to his predecessor, Les Chettle. Nonetheless, Thews was up to the challenge and began compiling evidence to support his client. He clearly intended to give Gonzales a fighting chance, no matter how recalcitrant his client was.

Thews had just come off a difficult murder case in Oakland's Superior Court. It concerned a nurse's aide, Esther Jones, who had been hit in the back by a stray bullet from a drive-by shooting while walking to her job at an Oakland disabled adults center. According to the prosecutor in the case, twenty-four-year-old

Lonnie Weathers and a friend had been chasing another vehicle driven by a man who owed them money. Weathers was the passenger as the high-speed chase ensued. Along the route, he pulled out an assault rifle, aimed it out the window and fired several bullets. None of the bullets hit the intended target, but one of the bullets struck Jones in the back, killing her.

Thews knew he had a tough case, but he put his client, Lonnie Weathers, on the stand and had him describe how he was nowhere near the scene of the crime at the time. He said he was having his car detailed in an auto shop. Unfortunately for Weathers, the prosecutor had an eyewitness who did put him at the scene of the crime, firing the fatal bullet out the window. That was the clincher as far as the jury was concerned. They found Weathers guilty as charged.

But at least Thews was able to stave off the prosecution's attempt to see first-degree murder charges brought against Weathers. The prosecutor had cited a section of law, known as "transferred intent," which stated that a defendant is guilty of first-degree murder if he intends to kill someone, and by mistake ends up taking the life of someone else. In the end, the jury bought Thews's defense that the crime was neither premeditated nor involved transferred intent. They found Weathers guilty of second-degree murder, which brought fifteen years to life, rather than something much worse.

Albert Thews told an *Oakland Tribune* reporter, "I was disappointed by their decision, but pleased they did not find first-degree murder."

Thews certainly hoped for even better results in the Benjamin Gonzales case, which promised to be a very intense and trying experience.

Meanwhile, the new deputy district attorney on the case, Morris Jacobson, who would be trying Gonzales for the murder of Barbara Muszalski, had just come off a difficult murder trial himself. It was a case of mistaken identity, kidnaping, torture and murder. On August 3, 1995, Miltonous Kingdom and two other men were convinced that William Highsmith, Jr., had stolen a car they owned that contained thousands of dollars' worth of illicit drugs in the trunk. They lured Highsmith to a West Oakland liquor store and in front of witnesses forced him at gunpoint into the trunk of Kingdom's Oldsmobile. They drove Highsmith up into the Oakland hills, then made him walk one hundred yards into the woods. They ordered him to strip down to his underwear, and tied him to a tree. Then it really got ugly. They pulled out a pair of scissors and began stabbing him, torturing him for hours, as they demanded information about the stolen car.

When they realized that Highsmith knew nothing about the stolen car, Kingdom's friend, Aaron Cooper, pulled out a pistol and shot Highsmith in the head at point-blank range. His body wasn't discovered until thirteen days later by an East Bay Municipal Utilities District worker.

All three assailants were eventually caught

and put on trial at various times. The other
two men were found guilty and convicted of
first-degree murder and kidnapping. Now it
was Miltonous Kingdom's turn, and Morris Jacobson was the prosecutor. He drilled in on
the heinous nature of the crime and the complete innocence of the victim. Even though the
defense attorney vowed that Kingdom was the
wrong man, the jury bought prosecutor Jacobson's argument. They found Kingdom guilty of
first-degree murder without the possibility of
parole. Deputy D.A. Jacobson hoped for similar
results in the Benjamin Gonzales case.

In the months before trial, Deputy D.A. Jacobson was incredibly busy compiling the mountains of evidence against Gonzales. One of the
chief weapons in his arsenal would be photographs. He knew that as far as a jury is concerned, sometimes a picture is indeed worth a
thousand words. He assembled color photos of
Barbara Muszalski, alive and dead, murder and
autopsy photos of Dondi Johnson with her
burned body, and graphic photos of slaughtered
Yvonne Hausley in New York City. These were
some of the most horrifying photographs a juror
would ever see. (In fact, one juror would faint
and have to be revived after viewing the photos.)

There were also multiple photos of bloody inmate Darrell Oliver, whom Gonzales had attacked, and some of Gonzales's bloodied
ex-attorney, Les Chettle, as well. Jacobson assembled photos of crime scenes, photos of knives
and of Barbara Muszalski's bloody Chevy S-10

tailgate. By the time he was done, the photos alone would number nearly one hundred.

He also got the psychiatrists' reports admitted, especially the Patton State Hospital reports of how Gonzales had been faking mental incompetency. Morris Jacobson sought a motion to consolidate the Barbara Muszalski murder with the Les Chettle and Darrell Oliver attacks, to be one trial. This immediately brought Gonzales's defense attorney, Albert Thews, out of the box with a rebuttal.

Thews wrote, "This case [the Barbara Muszalski case] for the People relies almost entirely on circumstantial evidence and is relatively weak compared to the felony assault on the previous trial attorney as charged in Superior Court case #12499 and the misdemeanor assault upon Darrell Oliver.

"For the purpose of this motion, the court must know that Gonzales has failed to cooperate with counsel in developing a defense to the charges, although he may change his mind at a future date.

"Even though the offenses may be joinable under #954 of the Penal Code, the court must exercise its discretionary power and determine if such joinder will prejudice the defendant. Substantial prejudice to the defendant may be shown where a weak case is coupled with a strong one or when the nature of the charges is inflammatory. *People* vs. *Smallwood 1986*.

"The jurors may well find it difficult to maintain a reasonable doubt as to the weak case when presented with strong evidence. . . . For all the above reasons the motion of the prosecution to consolidate these cases for trial must be denied."

Judge Jeffrey Horner did not agree with Albert Thews's argument. He allowed the consolidation and Benjamin Gonzales's jury would hear about the attacks on Les Chettle and Darrell Oliver. If the jurors deduced from these attacks that Benjamin Gonzales was indeed a very violent individual, that was exactly what prosecutor Jacobson wanted.

Defense attorney Thews not only had his hands full with the prosecution's motions, he had his hands continually being tied by his client, Benjamin Gonzales, as well. True to form, Gonzales absolutely refused to help in his defense. He argued with Thews, cussed him out and more often than not refused to answer any questions at all. On one occasion before entering court in a preliminary matter, Gonzales smeared himself with his own feces. On top of everything else, Thews had to worry if Gonzales might switch from noncooperation to downright violence.

Meanwhile, behind everyone's back, Gonzales was proving once again what a true con artist he could be. He talked a jail chaplain named Lynch into granting him phone privileges. But Gonzales didn't use the privileges to call his lawyer or family; he used the phone to stalk Nurse Sandi Nakamura at Patton State Hospital by telephone!

According to investigator Kathy Boyovich, at some point Chaplain Lynch became aware of

Gonzales's trying to contact Nakamura, but it didn't matter. Gonzales had convinced Lynch that he was in love with the woman. "He was a great bullshitter," according to Boyovich, "and could convince a lot of people into believing almost anything. He had this whiny kind of self-deprecating style, and people got sucked into believing he was harmless. Lynch was one of those people."

In fact, Chaplain Lynch not only let Gonzales abuse the jail phone privileges, he helped him by giving him easier access to the phones. He liked to believe in the good side of human nature. Unfortunately, in the case of Benjamin Gonzales, there wasn't much of a good side left.

On January 15, 1998, Gonzales called Patton State Hospital and tried to contact Nakamura. The following conversation later came to light.

Patton employee: "What's her name?"
Gonzales: "Her name is Sandi Nakamura."
Patton employee: "Sandi Nakamura. And what is your name?"
Gonzales: "Uh, tell her, uh, uh, tell her it's from Nick, and tell her, oh, oh, please only give her the message."
Patton employee: "Well . . ."
Gonzales: "And, only tell her where it's from, and tell her what time could I call her because, she's gonna be subpoenaed before the twentieth, and I'm tryin' to stop it. And tell her there's no way . . ."
Patton employee: "I'll ask her to give me the

details on this. Uh, call me Saturday and let's see what we could do."

Gonzales: "Okay, if . . ."

Patton employee: "Saturday noon, or afternoon, or evening."

Gonzales: "Uh, you know I'm not sure. It depends on my rotation. When I come out too, and that depends on when the next guy goes to court or whatever."

Patton employee: "Yeah."

Gonzales: "Hey, but if she's not there, Saturday, would she be there Sunday? Do you think you could try Sunday, if she's not there Saturday?"

Patton employee: "Well, we'll see, but I can't be making too many calls because this is Los Angeles."

Gonzales: "Uh-huh."

Patton employee: "And, it's very far away from here, and it's expensive."

Gonzales: "Okay."

Patton employee: "But, I'll do what I can."

Gonzales: "I very much, uh, appreciate . . ."

Patton employee: "What is the U.S. Marshall's number, do you know?"

Gonzales: "Okay, just a minute. Let me ask the officer just now, okay. Just a second. I think he might cut me off. If he does, I'll try to get back to you just . . ."

And then Gonzales was cut off.

When Sandi Nakamura found out that Benjamin Gonzales was trying to contact her, she became afraid and changed her phone number.

But this did not stop Gonzales in his obsession with her, or his trying to contact her by phone. He took the unprecedented step of jabbing a pencil into his midsection so he could get a trip to Highland Hospital. Phone security was much more lax at the hospital and he used this to advantage in trying to contact Nakamura. He also used an elaborate ruse of calling a neighbor in the area where his mom lived to try to set up a three-way call, where the person would contact Sandi, and then he could join in the conversation. Nothing was too elaborate or outlandish in his pursuit of Sandi Nakamura.

By late January 1998, he not only had an unwitting ally in Chaplain Lynch, he brought into his fold a very willing accomplice named Cindy, who was the girlfriend of another prisoner whom Gonzales knew. He had conned her into believing that Sandi Nakamura was just as much in love with him as he was with her. He relied upon Cindy's already antagonistic attitude toward prison authorities.

Gonzales's conversation with her about Nurse Sandi became very agitated on January 31, 1998. On that date, he had somehow made it through to Nakamura's new number and heard her voice. But a deputy was hovering nearby and he didn't get to talk to Sandi. When she hung up, it sent him into a frenzy. He immediately called his friend Cindy. He was so wound up, he kept getting dates and chronology all mixed up into one bundle.

Gonzales: "Hello, Cindy."
Cindy: "Yes [unintelligible]."

Gonzales: "How you doing? Uh, uh, are you awake?"

Cindy: "Yes."

Gonzales: "Oh, I'm sorry, girl. You wouldn't believe what, what I'm goin' through, and everything else with, uh, trying to get you. You know . . . Sandi, Sandi was on the phone this morning."

Cindy: "Uh-huh."

Gonzales: "And she thought it was the media. So, she said, so she said she wasn't there. And the deputy's talking to me at the same time, and I had the phone turned upside down, for, I wouldn't talk to her on the phone . . . and Sandi's thinking, Sandi's thinking, Sandi's thinking, Sandi's thinking it's the media, the lady from the media, and she's trying to say she's not there. And when I heard Sandi's voice . . . but the deputy's over here telling me he's gonna cut me off, and I'm over here tryin' to tell him please not to cut me off."

Cindy: "Yeah."

Gonzales: "And, then by the time that happened, Sandi already left off the phone. So, she, so she, right away, and so she thought the whole thing was that she was talkin' to the media. You know what I'm sayin'? So, that's why she said that and, and, then when I, and then when I, uh, uh, uh, then, then they said that, uh, Sandi wasn't there or San, there's no such person as Sandi there, you know and, and then she's not there. You know so [unintelligible] and you know I begged the deputies this morning. I said, I wasn't gonna get to call, you know what I had to do right now just to call you right now at this time?"

Cindy: "What?"

Gonzales: "I had to plan to stick a pencil in my stomach. To call you at this time."

Cindy: "Oh."

Gonzales: "Yeah, I had to, but see you're gonna, you're gonna [unintelligible] because see, uh, during New Year . . . New Year's I had my surgery on my stomach. They cut my stomach wide open 'cause I stuck a pencil in my stomach to talk to Sandi."

Cindy: "Oh, really?"

Gonzales: "Yeah. I know this sounds . . . I didn't think they were gonna do that. I thought the damn . . . there's just gonna be a little puncture wound, and uh, you know they're gonna just, just, you know, give me one stitch or two stitches and that was it, right?"

Cindy: "Uh-huh."

Gonzales: "Well, they said, 'You gotta go to surgery.' I said, 'What?' 'Surgery,' and then I said, 'You gotta be kidding?' They said no. And, the next thing I know, I'm under and when I woke up, I thought it was gonna be a little wound, right?"

Cindy: "Yeah."

Gonzales: When I woke up they split my whole stomach wide open. I said, 'God damn, just for a fuckin' phone call.' You know I'm tellin' you, girl, I'm goin' through a whole buncha changes. I got this big ol' scar now from my chest all the way past my belly button just for a phone call."

Then Gonzales cooked up a plan for Cindy to get in touch with Nakamura. She was to pretend she was from Chaplain Lynch's office and make contact with her. He also wanted Cindy to find out Sandi's home phone number. Amazingly, Cindy agreed.

For the rest of the call, Gonzales whined about his current medical condition.

Gonzales: "Oh, God, I've been awake all night. I'm stressin' real bad. I threw up two, two times last night."

Cindy: "Huh."

Gonzales: "I threw up two times last night."

Cindy: "What's wrong with you?"

Gonzales: "Oh, I got hella nerves. I'm drinking coffee, coffee, coffee, uh, and I couldn't eat. You know I didn't eat the whole day yesterday. I didn't eat, I didn't. I didn't the day before that, only a little bit of fruit, and then last night I knew I was gonna call Sandi now, and what happened? I threw up. But anyway, listen. I wanna do this as fast as possible 'cause I only got a little bit of time out here."

Cindy: "Okay."

Gonzales: "I know she is there today, girl. I know her work schedule. And if all of this doesn't work out, then I'll just have to do it myself. There's no way around it."

Gonzales gave Cindy various instructions how to get through to Patton State Hospital.

Gonzales: "She [Sandi] has a small break and everything else, but the break room is right there, right next to the office. . . . She's always accepted [a call] from the Chaplain. She always gets on the phone. Just try your best. If Sandi answers the phone, I'll be able to say something right away myself." [As part of a three-way call].

A short time later, Cindy did call Patton State Hospital and try to reach Sandi Naka-mura. She said she was calling from Chaplain Lynch's office as instructed. But the person at Patton on the other end of the line was wary. He kept asking for Cindy's name, and she kept putting him off. Then the employee asked for her telephone number, and she evaded him on this also. In fact, the employee at Patton asked Cindy for her phone number a half dozen times until Cindy became concerned and hung up.

But Benjamin Gonzales wasn't through with Cindy just yet. On February 24 at 2:05 P.M., he was back on the line with her.

Gonzales: "Bad news."
Cindy: "What?"
Gonzales: "Uh, you know [unintelligible] tellin' me about how the D.A. wants to put my head on the wall and he said that I'm gonna—"

Cindy: "He's not fair. He's a fool."

Gonzales: "He, he, he said you're a big old prize and everybody's been talkin' about you, he said, and, and, and you know they . . ."

Cindy: "You know what? I have a good mind to call him and ask him what's going on with you."

Gonzales: "Oh, my gosh."

Cindy: "Yeah."

Gonzales: "My lawyer wouldn't say a word too."

Cindy: "But I'm just sayin' to let him know that you have people that are on the outside at [unintelligible]."

Gonzales: "Yeah, the only thing he would, the only thing he would try and do is get you to go and testify at my trial and say somethin' like that. . . ."

Cindy: [Unintelligible.]

Gonzales: "Oh, shit, just a minute. Okay, oh, good. This mean guy gave me five minutes just now. He shined the light on me. [Everything's] locked down two minutes ago. Oh, God."

Cindy: "Okay?"

Gonzales: "Yeah, I hear you, but see they didn't—"

Cindy: "Now you gotta listen to me when I tell you these things, all right?"

Gonzales: "Yeah, I hear you, girl, but see they beat me down twice already. So bad I couldn't walk for three days."

Cindy: "What?"

Gonzales: "Yeah, I'm tellin' you, girl. They knocked me out; they knocked out one of my teeth. I have tendinitis [*sic*] now—you know where there's ringing in my ear. They beat me in the head so bad."

Cindy: "Why don't you go to the doctor?"

Gonzales: "Oh, the doctor said, you know, I've been hit so many times in the head that I'll probably have the tendinitis [*sic*] all my life. I have the ringing in my ears now."

Cindy: "Like [Muhammed] Ali."

Gonzales: "Yeah."

Cindy: "From boxin' and stuff, and then your memory gets bad."

Gonzales: "Oh, man . . ."

Cindy: "You could have some kind of blood clot in your brain. Why don't you have some X rays?"

Gonzales: "Yeah."

Cindy: "Why don't you put in for that? Will you do that for me?"

Gonzales: "Yeah, I'll, I'll, I'll . . . I'm still seeing the doctor."

Cindy: "I want you to put in for X rays on your head."

Gonzales: "Yeah, I hear you, girl. Hey, girl, I need to say something to you before they cut me off."

Cindy: "Say it."

Gonzales: "The thing is, do you think right now I could call Sandi's work?"

Cindy: "I'll only do this once."

Gonzales: "Okay, but . . ."

Cindy: "Once."

Gonzales: "You, you, you, do me a favor. From now on call me Tony, okay?"

Cindy: "Why?"

Gonzales: "I haven't used Ben in twenty years. I been using Tony."

Cindy: "I'll call you Tony, if I can remember it."

Then Gonzales gave her Sandi Nakamura's new phone number.

Gonzales: "If Sandi's on the line, I will give you extra time."

Cindy: "Uh-huh."

Gonzales: "Oh, I'm gonna say 'George.' She should get on the phone if I say 'George.' "

Cindy: "Okay, because every time you do that, when he asks you, that's when you get stuck and that's where you get messed up."

Gonzales: "Okay?"

Cindy: "Okay, baby."

Cindy then tried calling Sandi at Patton State Hospital.

Cindy: "She's not there."

Gonzales: "Just let it ring a few more times."

Cindy: "I'm gonna let it ring a few more times, but when you disrespect me like that, I hate it."

Gonzales: "What did I do, girl?"

Cindy: "I'm gonna tell you in a minute."

Gonzales: "Damn."

Cindy: "[She's] not there."

Gonzales: "Okay."

Cindy: "Why be so anxious to get in touch with Sandi?"

Gonzales: "Girl, I wanna get out of here. I wanna go home."

Then he suddenly got angry at Sandi.

Gonzales: "She's the most revengeful mother-fucker there is. She thinks, she thinks . . . Uh, believe me, girl, I love her more than anything in the world, but she is playing an ugly game. You know I could be so many things to her. I could get her fired. I could get her locked up. I could burn her." [Kill her.]

Cindy: "That's stupid."

Gonzales: "I could get her in prison for at least ten years. Oh, I could, oh, I could, oh, I could, do her."

Cindy: "Right. And you're being real cool with this. What she's doin' is just not [unintelligible]. You know what? You're gonna have to give her a little example. You're gonna have to shake her up. Shake up her job."

Gonzales: "Yeah, that's what I'm tellin' you, girl."

Cindy: "Maybe at first I didn't agree with you."

Gonzales: "Yeah."

Cindy: "But, see, I don't like what she's doin' to you."

Gonzales: "Yeah."

Cindy: "It's wrong."

Gonzales: "I got a million things I want to tell you, and thanks for being on my side, girl, and you're the only inspiration I got."

Cindy: "Well, I love you."

Gonzales: "You know what, girl, I have room in my heart for you, believe it or not, and that's a real strange thing for me to say to anybody."

Cindy: "Thank you. I know the same thing, the same thing I said to you."

Gonzales: "I'm getting off. . . ."

Cindy: "Okay. Be good and don't get in trouble."

Gonzales: "Okay, 'bye, 'bye, girl."

Cindy: " 'Bye, 'bye."

Incredible as it may seem, Benjamin Gonzales had just threatened over the jail house phone to kill a woman who was spurning his advances. And he got another woman to agree that he was right!

Gonzales wasn't done abusing his telephone privileges yet. In fact, the next woman he conned was even more puzzling than Cindy. Her name was Carole, and she was not only a bright, articulate woman, she was part of a Catholic relief organization that visited and corresponded with prisoners. Before long, the suave side of Benjamin Gonzales had her just as fooled as he had Cindy. What was even more dangerous, she came to visit him in his cell. Since Gonzales always stashed hidden weapons away, she never knew how lucky she was to survive these visits unscathed. Just one incident where she angered him and he lost his temper might have cost her her life.

Carole lived in an upscale part of the Bay Area with her husband and always believed in helping others. She set up an organization in the local area that reached out to prisoners. It even won a humanitarian cause award. Benjamin Gonzales particularly appealed to her because of his quiet and polite manner when he was around her. He seemed to be suffering a lot from his AIDS problem, and she was only too willing to help in making sure he made his doctor's appointments and other matters.

But eventually she stepped over the line and became an instrument of his psychosis. She had recently been on a vacation in Mexico with her husband and Gonzales asked for a photograph of her. What he got was probably beyond his wildest imagination. She sent him a photo of her lounging on the beach, wearing a bikini. She smiled at the camera in a provocative way and leaned back in what was once called "a cheesecake shot."

Even more amazing than this, Gonzales asked for an article of her clothing to keep with him. Carole sent him a swatch of a dress bathed in perfume. Just what Gonzales did with her revealing photo and piece of perfume-bathed dress in the privacy of his cell can only be guessed at.

She wrote him a very revealing letter on April 30, 1998, explaining just how she felt about him. It read:

Dear Ben, First I want to tell you how *moved* I was by the first two pages of the 'big' letter. Your ability to describe your feelings is *awesome* and I feel honored that you chose to share them with me. Tears came to my eyes, and for the first time I *really* felt "appreciated" by you! Thank you for your courage to trust and be vulnerable.

I'm glad you sent me copies of the complaints and I *promise* you I will *act* on this and make a loud noise of protest until I am heard. I have put calls to three different agencies regarding getting an AIDS advocate with legal experience to come to the jail to talk to you, or [at] least accept your collect phone calls. Unfortunately, I had to leave voice-mail messages for every one of them, and I'm waiting for return calls. . . . Hope you like the items you requested. [The photo and piece of perfumed dress she sent.] You will continue to be in my thoughts, and heart and prayers.
Love, Carole.

Even more puzzling than this letter was the fact that Carole, who should have known better about prisoners by now, became part of his obsessive scheme to phone Sandi Nakamura at Patton State Hospital. She not only was a pawn in his scheme, she became a willing accomplice. She used the excuse of being in Chaplain Lynch's office to set Ben up with the phone, or to relay messages to Nakamura's workplace.

This incredible state of affairs went on until

Deputy District Attorney Morris Jacobson got wind of her attachment to Gonzales. He still didn't know about all the phone calls, but a cell search revealed her "cheesecake" photo and swatch of perfumed dress. This spurred a phone call between Carole and Gonzales on June 9.

Gonzales: "Hi, Carole, what are you doing?"

Carole: "Hi, how are you? I haven't talked to you. . . ."

Gonzales: "How come it took me forever to contact you?"

Carole: "Well, because I can't call . . . I mean I can't write there."

Gonzales: "But all you gotta do is put John Doe and, and . . ."

Carole: "No, Chaplain Lynch said it wouldn't be in my best interests 'cause they would intercept the letters."

Gonzales: "Yeah, but if you put John Doe just like my partner did a long time ago, when he was going through the same thing as here, it came through with no problems."

Carole: "Yes, well . . ."

Gonzales: "I mean all they do is read the envelope on the outside and that's that."

Carole: "Well, I mean we would have to come up with some name or address that wasn't the same as mine, you know."

Then about her photo.

Gonzales: "They look, like, you know [unintelligible], pictures and whatnot."

Carole: "Yeah. I know that. Of course, you have some guilt in that for asking me to do something."

Then about the threat by the deputy D.A. to make an enlargement of her photo to be used in court.

Gonzales: "Yeah, I know, I know. Well, at least, put it this way. In court, you'll be life size."

Carole: "Oh, come on. I am not gonna go to court. If it's true that the district attorney has my picture. I am not even showing up."

Gonzales: "There's no way you could avoid that."

Carole: "They'd have to subpoena me, sorry."

Gonzales: "I know. It's just a life-sized picture though, I mean."

Carole: "Oh, come on. No, and Chaplain Lynch is driving me crazy on that."

Gonzales: "No, no."

Carole: "It's not funny, it is not funny."

Gonzales: "It's funny to me because, I know you're goin' crazy over there about nothing."

Carole: "It shouldn't be funny to you."

Gonzales: "I mean if you were fat and ugly, and all this other shit. I could imagine."

Carole: "No, no, I'm talking about . . ."

Gonzales: "I know what you're thinking."

Carole: "I'm talking about being banned from there."

Gonzales: "Yeah . . . oh, that part's not funny. The part I'm laughing about is the blowing up [of the photo]."

Carole: "Well, I know, but that's just a joke you guys created."

Then Gonzales talked about his upcoming court date.

Gonzales: "It's on the twenty-ninth."
Carole: "Oh, gosh. Well, I'm gonna be . . . I don't know if Chaplain Lynch had a chance to tell you . . . my husband and I are gonna go on vacation. And we're gonna be out of state. And so I don't want you calling the service."
Gonzales: "Hum."
Carole: "And it costs us money every time you even call the service and they answer it, and so anyway it's gonna be from . . . we're gonna be out of the state between Sunday, June 21, through Monday, June 29."
Gonzales: "My, my, my court date, huh?"
Carole: "I know, well, I had no idea that was gonna be your court date. Anyway, I don't wanna come down there if the district attorney has that picture of me."
Gonzales: "Believe me, that's the best sign in the world. If he's trippin' over that, that means that they don't have nothing on me."
Carole: "I hope that, they don't have anything on you, if they have to scrape up my picture."
Gonzales: "Yeah, that's good . . . that's a very good sign. . . ."

Carole: "How are you feeling healthwise?"

Gonzales: "Oh, I'm screwed up real bad, you know. I got these damn things that look like I got the measles."

Carole: "Where?"

Gonzales: "All over my body."

Carole: "Like a rash?"

Gonzales: "Well, it looks like the measles or some shit."

Carole: "Hum, have you . . . well, has someone looked at it?"

Gonzales: "Nobody."

Carole: "Well, why don't you have it looked at? Show your AIDS doctor."

Gonzales: "I been tryin' for a month now. He won't come."

Carole: "You haven't been in to see him for a month?"

Gonzales: "I haven't seen him for a month now and they keep . . . I was supposed to see him ten days ago and then he didn't call me."

Carole: "Well, what happened?"

Gonzales: "I don't know. I, I, I complained about it, and complained about it and nobody came. And they said, well, he'll see you when he's got time. They cut me off from my Motrin, my Tagamet. They cut me off my Ensure drink. They cut me off I forget what else."

Carole: "Well, who is 'they,' who cut you off?"

Gonzales: "My sinus med . . . my thing ran out because the doctor hasn't seen me for so long to renew the damn shit . . . I mean most of the nurses don't care . . . and I just got two fillings filled in my teeth yesterday and my teeth is killing me. I have no Motrin. See, I told 'em, 'Look, this is fuckin' shit on why I stay on the pills in the first place anyway, because you do this kinda shit.' . . . And I said, 'Oh, I been so damn crazy with this tooth.' "

Carole: "Are you getting the right AIDS medication?"

Gonzales: "I, I, I, I don't know. They, they, they . . . I haven't seen no test in over two months. . . . There's something real wrong with me because I'm getting this . . . it's not a rash, it's something else . . . little, little, little bumps on my sides and now my back, and now my stomach."

Carole: "Well, are you taking something new you didn't used to take?"

Gonzales: "Nothing, nothing."

Carole: "Wow, it sounds like an allergic reaction."

Gonzales: "They itch like hell. . . . Then they go away and leave like scars. . . . The damn shit is spreading like crazy. It's just going nuts on me."

Carole: "Wow."

Then Gonzales's thoughts turned back to his obsession with Sandi Nakamura.

Gonzales: "I still haven't talked to Sandi, do you believe it?"

Carole: "Yeah, yeah, I believe it."

Gonzales: "It took me forever to get her other number. Like 'cause I couldn't get to the phone. And then when I finally did get it, that other guy, my enemy, called her and she changed her damn number again."

Carole: "Unh-huh."

Gonzales: "And then I had to go and contact all these fuckin' people again to get a second new number, and then when I got the second new number and now I can't get through to the person who has the second new number. I'm goin' fuckin' crazy with this shit. And you know I don't want to be mean to her [Sandi]. I, I, I don't wanna be mean to her or anything. . . . She's gonna be subpoenaed, I think, whether she likes it or not. . . . It's all logical that they're gonna do it. Nobody else knows me [like she does]. They know I love her. Everybody knows I love her. You know what I'm saying. They don't know the seriousness of it and all . . . but they're looking for . . . I mean, I don't have any weak links in my chain. And they always attack the weak links. So I'm willing to sell my soul too for that girl, just so nobody would even hurt her, just even her feelings. . . . If she wants to screw herself, I'm gonna let her. Well, that's her fate. All I wanna do is talk to her."

Gonzales and Carole then got into an argument about whether she had letters from Sandi to him. She claimed she never got any letters from either Sandi, or him, that he had sent to her for safekeeping.

Gonzales: "Listen to the history of this and that way you'll understand."

Carole: "What is the point of telling me the history? I never had those letters."

Gonzales: "Carole, you . . . I sent 'em to you."

Carole: "I have never gotten any letters from Sandi or from you to Sandi. I've never seen them."

Gonzales: "Ca, Ca, Carole, they're, they're . . ."

Carole: "Ben, please believe me, I have no reason to lie to you."

Gonzales: "You won't listen to me, you won't listen to me. . . . I'm only going by what you told me, Carole. I'm repeating your own words."

Carole: "Ben, you don't remember what I said two weeks ago."

Gonzales: "That ain't the most important . . ."

Carole: "I don't even remember what I said two weeks ago."

Gonzales: "That's the most important thing."

Carole: "Good-bye, Ben, you've done it again. You've fuckin' pissed me off, good-bye."

Gonzales: "What, what . . . fuckin' idiot, fuckin' idiot!"

It can be imagined what Benjamin Gonzales thought about another woman hanging up on him, especially when it came to his obsession with Sandi Nakamura. But that was the least of Carole's problems at the time. The deputy district attorney did indeed have the photo of her sunning herself on the beach, as well as the swatch of perfumed dress that she had sent to Gonzales, and he intended to use them in court. It wouldn't be long before he had all the tapes of her phone conversations as well.

But at the moment Deputy D.A. Morris Jacobson had another very important date on his agenda. On July 6, 1998, Benjamin Gonzales and his lawyer, Albert Thews, took their last stab at having him declared incompetent to stand trial. Gonzales pulled out all the stops on this one. If he wasn't crazy, he was sure trying his best to make Judge Jeffrey Horner think he was. The competency hearing was not held at the courthouse, but rather in a secure area of the North County Jail. The only court people in attendance were Judge Horner, Deputy D.A. Jacobson and his assistant, Kathy Boyovich, defense attorney Thews, a court reporter, a court clerk and two bailiffs.

Albert Thews got the proceedings rolling by asking Benjamin Gonzales his name. But even a simple question received no straight answer from Gonzales. He said, "My name is Bennie the Jet, Andrew, Robert, Roberto—something like that."

Then he immediately started in on his whining. "I didn't sleep last night. They woke me up real fast and they said I had to go to court. I put on my clothes and they took me in another room, messed up my hair and took my clothes and everything else. I didn't get a chance to wash or comb my hair. They rushed me. Nobody let me do anything. They chained me up real fast. I haven't had no sleep and I was trying to sleep on the floor right now."

When Albert Thews asked him why he was sent to Patton State Hospital, Gonzales answered, "To get out of the dome."

Then he elaborated. "The dome—it's a dome I been under for a long time. It keeps me in one place. I could feel the pressure in it . . . we're light. We're all energy. And you know there's only one way to give you my light, and that's for somebody else to take my light from me or to make me wear something or believe something when I know I could hear something else."

Albert Thews asked him if the dome was at the North County Jail. Gonzales answered, "It's everywhere."

Asked why he thought he was incarcerated in the North County Jail, he answered, "For trying to leave the dome."

Thews wanted to know about what control the dome had over him. Gonzales responded, "It's not the control the dome has over me. It's the control everyone else in the dome. See, out of the dome, everybody can be themselves. But if I'm locked up or shut out like when I used to be tied to a pole and stuff. . . ." And then he lost his train of thought.

Albert Thews asked, "Are you in jail for stabbing your lawyer with a pencil in March of 1995?"

Gonzales answered, "Aren't you my lawyer?"

"I'm your lawyer now. Did you have another lawyer before me?"

"It doesn't seem like it. It seems like I know you for a long time."

Asked if he was aware of the charges against him for stabbing Les Chettle with a pencil, Gonzales said, "Can you repeat that again? I was hearing something else at the same time you're talking. I'm trying to separate right now. . . . I'm hearing a couple of other people. They're not people, but they're voices. I feel funny saying it because I only told the chaplain. I never told anybody else. I told a nextdoor neighbor one time, and they told my dad."

Thews said, "Mr. Gonzales, give me a yes or no."

He replied, "No, I'm not stabbing anyone."

"Are you aware that you're charged with the murder of Barbara Muszalski in April of 1992?"

"No."

"Do you have any drug charges pending against you?"

"I'm not too sure. For the acid— for the PCP. Nobody's asked me."

"Have you heard of a plea of not guilty by reason of insanity?"

"Yeah, yeah."

"What does that mean to you?"

"I get . . . I get . . . I get . . . I'll have to take my medication again or be under the dome or take a chance of hearing something or not hearing something. I don't feel anything."

Albert Thews asked him the days of the week and months of the year and Gonzales got them all right. But when asked what year it was, he claimed the year to be 1980.

About time in general, Gonzales said, "If you look at the clock, sometimes you can see the clock stop and time stop. If you look at it like under the dome. If I'm locked up somewhere or tied up . . . I'm going into the tunnel. The tunnel goes into the light. There's two different lights. There's a dark light and a bright light. I don't want to go into the dark light."

Thews asked him what happens when you go into the dark light.

"[It's like] when my dad tied me up and beat me up. I felt at peace and I could hear my mother calling me. I knew then if I could hear my voice I could go back into the light. I don't have to be here . . . I could never die. There's no way I could die."

Thews asked, "Are you alive now?"

Gonzales responded, "If you want to call it that."

"Will you ever die?"

"I'll never die."

"Will you live forever?"

"Yeah. I'm somewhere else. I'll go into the other world. I survived a long time. I could see his energy [pointing at Deputy D.A. Jacobson]. I could see hers over there [pointing at Jacobson's female investigator, Kathy Boyovich]. She's the one who knows what I'm thinking."

Wanting to get back to court proceedings, Thews asked, "Direct your attention to the gentleman seated up at the front wearing the black robe . . . do you know what he does?"

"Yeah, he's going to get the energy from them [pointing at Deputy D.A. Jacobson and Kathy Boyovich]. See, everybody feeds off everybody else's different energy. He [the judge] feeds off nobody's energy. He sits in the chair like a stone chair. I used to think he was God, but he's not God. He's going to feed off [Jacobson's] light and the lady's light."

Asked by Thews what the purpose of the defense attorney was, Gonzales answered, "You're trying to get my energy by helping that guy [pointing at Jacobson]."

Thews asked, "Have you lost your energy?"

"No, because I won't give it up."

"Now, Mr. Gonzales, if I told you that the man seated to my right is the district attorney of Alameda County, do you believe that?"

Gonzales answered, "I'll listen to anything you say. But that's why I don't talk to nobody because I let them believe what they want to believe. What I know—I know. What other people want me to believe, I just go along with."

"Earlier, Mr. Gonzales, you pointed to a person who's typing on a machine. And you said that he had something to do with energy under the dome. What does he do?"

"He's a new energy. He's learning everybody else's energy. He's helping to assist everybody's energy. He's not trying to hurt me. He's not trying to do anything."

Albert Thews said, "If I told you that he was taking down all that is said, would you believe me?"

"No," Gonzales replied.

"Mr. Gonzales, earlier in my questioning you pointed at the lady who is the clerk of the court. What does this lady do in the courtroom?"

"I don't know, but I like her TV screen." [Computer monitor.]

"Does the lady clerk do anything in the courtroom?"

"Yes, she's trying to take my energy, but not personally."

Then Thews pointed to Judge Jeffrey Horner. "I'm pointing over to the gentleman who is wearing the black robe here. If I call him a judge, would you believe me?"

"I'll believe anything you want to tell me," Gonzales responded.

Unable to resist this straight line by Gonzales, Thews quipped, "All right, he's a judge. What does a judge do?"

"He's trying to feed off his energy [Morris Jacobson's]. That is like a shark eating something and then the catfish coming and eating the leftovers. In a different way it's light. It's just like the rays of the sun. We're all part of the sun. There's a bright light and the dark light. The bright light is to be part of where we came from. Dark light is to take the energy from people."

"Mr. Gonzales, do you know what we are doing now in this courtroom?"

"Yes, trying to take my energy."

"If I told you we were holding a hearing to see if you could help your attorney in the defense of the cases against you, would you believe me?"

"I'll believe anything you want . . . but what you want me to think and what I know are two different things."

Gonzales pointed at Morris Jacobson's pretty investigator, Kathy Boyovich, and said, "I'm making her nervous."

In fact, one witness of the proceedings said that Boyovich was piling up law books so that Gonzales couldn't look directly at her with his insane stare.

Albert Thews asked, "Can you hear what the lady in the courtroom is thinking?"

"Yeah, she's afraid."

"And who is she afraid of?"

"She's afraid of me."

"Tell us why she is afraid of you."

"Because she can't take my light. I could hear her. That's why I put paper in my ears. Sometimes, because I don't want to hear nothing. I don't want to hear them all day long. When I wake up, I hear them."

Shifting gears, Thews asked, "At Patton State Hospital did they tell you what a courtroom was?"

Gonzales answered, "Doesn't seem like it."

To the questions whether they told him about judges, district attorneys, defense attorneys, court reporters and court clerks, he had the same answer—"Doesn't seem like it."

"Do you know what it means to have criminal charges against you?" Thews asked.

Gonzales replied, "Yeah. It means they don't want to do something [for you] because you're addicted to something. It's the same thing when you find yourself somewhere and you're not quite sure how you got there. Or you're dressed different . . . or the furniture has moved around. I'm under the dome. I'm never going to get out of the dome. I've only been out of the dome a little while and that's because I saw my light. And I was trying to be at peace."

Thews asked him several times if he knew that he was his attorney and that he was trying to help him. But Gonzales kept turning the question in on itself and asked, "Are you asking me or telling me?"

Finally Thews said, "I am your attorney against any criminal charges—do you understand that?"

"You're my attorney?" Gonzales finally said. "Okay."

Albert Thews couldn't resist another chance for levity. He said, "Sold, huh? Okay. I'm your attorney. Will you cooperate with me in defending against any charges brought to you by the district attorney?"

"Say that again. I was hearing something else. I'm trying to separate you and everything else."

"Okay. Who else are you hearing beside me?"

"I'm hearing Bennie the Jet, and the overseer, the overseer who I used to think was in charge of everything. But the chaplain told me the overseer reports to the guy that sits in the stone chair."

"The judge up there, is he overseeing?"

"No. I only seen shadows of him. I saw [his] shoulder one time. He's the guy in charge of everything."

"Mr. Gonzales, will you help me to defend against any criminal charges brought against you by the district attorney?"

"Every time somebody wants to help me, somebody wants something from me. What do you want from me? I don't have nothing to give you."

"I don't want anything from you, Mr. Gonzales. Will you help me to defend against any criminal charges brought against you?"

"Do you understand the light?"

"No."

"See, you're not being honest with me."

"Mr. Gonzales, tell me about the light."

"We're all part of the light. It's like the sun. Like a ray of sun. There's no heaven, and there's no hell. There's no God. We're all gods. Like the flower. We all take turns. We're all part of each other. When we all become part of each other, we all know what the other knows. We all feel what the other feels. We are all trying to be at peace and not be afraid. There's a light like the sun. And then there's a dark light. Once they take your light, you become a part of them. [He pointed at Deputy D.A. Jacobson.] He takes my light. Then after he feeds on a few people like me, then he'll allow her [his assistant] to feed on somebody else."

"Mr. Gonzales, what does the light have to do with the dome?"

"I'm not too sure. In the dome there's windows. And you can go to different places. It's just like when I did surgery on myself. I went into one of the windows, but I never would come out of the dome, because if I came out of the dome, I could see what everybody else looks like. And everybody else doesn't want me to see what they look like. I have stabbed myself nineteen times. I've done all kinds of things."

Finally Albert Thews was through trying to decipher Benjamin Gonzales's incoherent statements. It was Deputy D.A. Morris Jacobson's turn to try to delve into Gonzales's convoluted logic and his competency to stand trial—or lack thereof.

He started out by asking Gonzales about his contacts with counselor Carole. Jacobson asked, "Did you ask her to send you a photograph of her in a bikini bathing suit on a beach?"

"Her in a bikini?" Gonzales replied. "No, she always wears a lot of clothes."

"You ever discussed the business of the dome with any of the deputies in jail?"

"No, I already have trouble with them. Especially after I got beat up two times. Might have been more. They knocked out my tooth."

"Mr. Gonzales, do you often ask deputies to let you out of your cell to use the telephone?"

"I tried to call my mom and Carole most of the time."

"Have you ever tried to call Nurse Sandi [Nakamura] at Patton Hospital?"

"I don't have her phone number."

"You've tried though through third parties, haven't you? You call them to use a three-way call to try and contact Sandi at Patton State Hospital, right?"

"Sounds like something I would do."

"The business of being in and out of the dome, that's nothing that you have talked to psychiatrists or psychologists about, is it?"

"I've been outside the dome for a short time. . . . I know the weaker I get, the more easier it's going to get to take my energy from me. They come after me. Everybody comes after me. You're coming to [make] me weaker. I go to lay down, and still I hear the voices—"

Jacobson cut him off. "Mr. Gonzales, the first time you've discussed being in the dome was here today in court, correct?"

"No, I've told the chaplain."

Jacobson reiterated the fact that Gonzales knew that Albert Thews was his lawyer, had in fact called him by name. He also knew what deputies were, and also knew what a district attorney was. Gonzales got frustrated and whined, "You're asking me something with no sleep. I'm nervous."

Jacobson asked, "Would you prefer to take the opportunity to sleep? I don't want to ask you questions if you haven't had enough sleep."

Gonzales replied, "You can ask me anything

you want any time. Nothing is going to change. Nothing ever changes. That's why I watch things move. That's why you put me in a cell right now, when I can't tell the amount of time. I have no way of telling time. No way of seeing things move. That's why I run my water. Because you know if I run my water, you guys have to make the time go by. And I know these guys [the deputies] don't like it."

Jacobson pounced on Gonzales's supposed inability to tell time. He asked, "Don't you frequently ask the deputies, 'I should have a doctor's appointment tomorrow. Can you check the computer to see whether I'm on the list to go to Santa Rita for a doctor's appointment?' "

"No, they don't like me. I always have problems with them. I always argue with them. This morning I was yelling at them because I couldn't get my medication. I was pounding on the door."

Jacobson said, "Did you say something to a deputy last Wednesday afternoon when you got back from court about the fact that you were going to act up in regard to wiping fecal matter on a chair or your clothes?"

"Fecal matter? What's fecal matter?"

"Waste. Human waste."

"Shit?"

"Shit."

Gonzales whined, "They wouldn't let me wear my light clothes. See, the dark clothes keep them happy. To think I'm still going to the light. See, like the string around my neck. See, it has dark and it has gold in there. Light and dark. If they see the dark in it, they're going to be comfortable."

With that final explanation about light and dark, Morris Jacobson said, "No more questions, Your Honor."

In summing up their opinions about the rambling soliloquies they had just heard emanating from Benjamin Gonzales, Albert Thews had a very different version of his "reality" than Morris Jacobson did. Thews told the judge, "There are times when he's competent and times when he's not. Competency doesn't stay forever."

Jacobson responded, "This bizarre talk and all this garbage we heard is blatant malingering. If he wants to, he can choose to assist his attorney."

There was one more person who was about to put a nail in Benjamin Gonzales's "competency coffin." It was Dr. Jules Burstein. He told the court regarding the phone conversation with Carole, "These are conversations between the defendant [and Carole] that have no indication of mental, cognitive or psychiatric impairment. In fact, there's straightforward discussion about his case, his concerns, the frustrations of being locked up, some concerns about how his attorney was handling the case. What's notable about [the phone calls] is that there's nothing notable about them. They're just ordinary phone conversations from a man who is locked up. There's no evidence in his language of any kind of mental disorder."

As to the letter from Carole to Gonzales, Dr. Burstein said, "She says [to Gonzales], 'Your ability to describe your feelings is awesome, and I feel honored that you chose to share them with me.' Somebody who is supposed to be disorganized psychologically as to be viewed incompetent would not inspire that kind of admiration from someone writing him. Such a person would have a very difficult time writing a coherent letter."

Finally, Deputy D.A. Morris Jacobson asked Dr. Burstein, "In your review of the medical records, did you find any discussion whatsoever or any documentation of Mr. Gonzales describing a dome, D-O-M-E, being inside the dome or outside the dome, anything of that nature?"

Dr. Burstein responded, "If it was there, I don't recall it."

"How about anything related to a tunnel and a dark light and a light light?"

"I don't recall that either."

"Any claims of people taking his energy?"

"None that I recall."

"Anything of overseers sitting in stone chairs?"

"No."

"Based on all the information you have before you, how would you account for that type of behavior while [Benjamin Gonzales] testified here in court two days ago?"

Dr. Burstein responded, "My best assessment would be that one should conclude it's ridiculous posturing intended to convince the court that he's mentally disturbed."

In the end, Judge Jeffrey Horner agreed with Deputy D.A. Morris Jacobson and Dr. Jules Burstein. He said, "The defendant is a malingerer and has been ever since he first raised mental health claims."

The trial for the murder of Barbara Muszalski would go forward and Gonzales would not be going back to Atascadero or Patton State Hospital.

Finally in October 1998, the Gonzales trial was set to begin. Barbara Muszalski's daughter told a *San Francisco Chronicle* reporter, "It's been very frustrating. It's a big game for him. Our only consolation is that he's been in jail the whole time."

What she didn't know was that Gonzales was still creating absolute havoc in the jail. He talked back to jail personnel, he picked fights with other inmates who were within hearing distance and he went to extreme lengths to abuse phone privileges.

Still unaware that Gonzales's phone stalking of Nurse Sandi Nakamura had not ended, but rightfully fearful for security measures in his court, Judge Horner ordered a second bailiff to be present at all times while the court was in session. But Deputy D.A. Jacobson wanted even more. He wrote the judge a paper, *Points of Shackling Defendant.*

A defendant may be shackled during a trial if the court determines that there is a manifest need for such restraint. *People* vs. *Pride 1992*. Manifest need arises upon a showing of unruliness, an announced intention to escape or evidence of any nonconforming conduct which disrupts or would disrupt the judicial process if defendant were to be left unrestrained. . . . Defendant [Gonzales] while in custody, has engaged in a well-documented pattern of violent, abusive and defiant behavior. For example, he has assaulted at least two inmates, sending one to the hospital for eighteen stitches to the face and mouth. He beat and stabbed his former defense attorney in the courthouse stairwell, sending him to the hospital by ambulance. These attacks are frequent and premeditated.

Defendant has also been found in possession of numerous homemade stabbing weapons on his person, both on his way to court and in his cell on numerous occasions. He manufactured a key from a comb to his cell door lock that not only opened the door, but it defeated the electronic security monitoring system by making it appear that the door was locked.

He is often abusive and threatening toward inmates and jail staff. He is known to refuse to take directions from sheriff's deputies and jail staff and he has been dis-

ciplined on several occasions for not acting respectfully toward jail personnel.

Then Deputy D.A. Jacobson related new
revelations about more phone calls in Gonzales's attempts to reach Sandi Nakamura at
Patton State Hospital.

> Defendant has also gone to extreme
> lengths to manipulate access to telephones
> in order to continue his stalking of a psy-
> chiatric nurse at Patton State Hospital.
> Most notably he has engaged in multiple
> acts of self-mutilation by inserting sharp-
> ened objects into his stomach in order to
> get transferred to the hospital where he
> has unfettered access to the telephone.
> Further, defendant engages in other acts
> of disruptive inappropriateness in court.
> He has been known to pull his shirt over
> his face. On one occasion he smeared
> himself with fecal matter just before enter-
> ing the courtroom. . . . In the face of the
> known, actual and demonstrated danger
> that the defendant confronts us all with,
> this court must do all it can to ensure the
> physical safety to all people who set foot
> in the courtroom during the course of
> this trial. The jury, the witnesses, the court
> staff, the attorneys, the bailiffs and even
> the defendant himself will be immediately
> safer from violent attack if this court re-
> quires defendant to be, at minimum,

shackled at the feet and the hands and the waist.

On October 22, 1998, Judge Horner granted Deputy D.A. Jacobson's request.

All while Morris Jacobson was writing up his paper for restraint, Benjamin Gonzales was anything but restrained. When he was sent back from Highland Hospital, he still conned the Santa Rita Jail chaplain into letting him use the phone so he could stalk Sandi Nakamura at Patton State Hospital.

When Judge Jeffrey Horner finally got wind of all this phone stalking, he went through the roof. He brought both defense attorney Albert Thews and Deputy D.A. Morris Jacobson into his chambers and laid down the law. He said, "The defendant [Gonzales] has on a number of occasions injured himself specifically for the purpose of being transported to Highland Hospital for the specific purpose of being able to make telephone calls. In my judgment, these dangerous activities, stalking behavior and the like, are to use what has been perceived by the defendant to be overly lax telephone security at the hospital. This is going to stop."

He then ordered all doctors, nurses and sheriff's deputies to deny Benjamin Gonzales any and all telephone privileges.

Judge Horner went on to say, "If I learn that any doctor, nurse or other person has allowed telephone calls to Mr. Gonzales that violate this order, I will consider holding that person or persons in contempt of court, and that con-

tempt of court may involve sanctions such as
incarceration in jail or fines or both.

"The only exception of this is contacting his
own attorney, Albert Thews. Any telephone
contact with Mr. Thews must be dialed by sheriff's department personnel and only after sheriff's department personnel are certain that the
persons contacted are Albert Thews or his
staff.

"Finally the last order of court is that from
this moment forward, Mr. Gonzales is to have
no contact whatsoever with Chaplain Lynch. I
am in no way cutting off the defendant from
any contact with religious personnel. That is not
my intent at all. But I've heard enough evidence
here to indicate that Chaplain Lynch's behavior
in this was highly inappropriate and may have
been unlawful."

Defense attorney Albert Thews definitely had
his troubles as the case was coming to trial—
not the least of them being Benjamin Gonzales
himself. And Deputy D.A. Jacobson was putting
together a witness list that was a mile long.
There were to be seven witnesses from Los Angeles concerning the Dondi Johnson murder,
six witnesses from New York on the Yvonne
Hausley murder, and more than thirty witnesses from the Bay Area on the murder of
Barbara Muszalski, and the Darrell Oliver and
Les Chettle assaults.

Then there was Dr. Jules Burstein as well. He
had often been called upon to evaluate violent

criminals and give testimony in court. In the
present matter he was giving Benjamin Gonzales no pass. He called him, "A manipulative
sociopath who conned the doctors who found
him incompetent."

Even Judge Horner's comments in the pretrial hearings were making it into the newspapers as he discussed the unusual security
measures that would be in effect in his courtroom. He said, "This defendant is an extremely manipulative, inventive and devious
person. He is able to exploit even a momen-
tary lapse in security. I have never seen a more
manifest need for precautions."

Judge Horner sat in every juror's chair to
personally determine if there was a way to con-
ceal several feet of chains and locks beneath
Gonzales's clothing so the jurors would not
know he was wearing them. He decided that
the chains and locks could be concealed and
that the trial would take place under those
conditions.

The extraordinary precautions didn't stop
there. Judge Horner ordered that there must
always be an empty chair between Gonzales
and his attorney, Albert Thews. This in effect
put Thews closer to Deputy D.A. Jacobson than
it did his own client. And if Benjamin Gonzales
ever decided he wanted to talk to his lawyer,
the judge decided that the whole courtroom
would be evacuated first.

D.A. Jacobson was chiming in with the press
as well, about courtroom security. He told
David Holbrook of the *Valley Times,* "He [Gon-

zales] is persistent, he's tenacious, he's smart. This man is as dangerous as anybody will ever see. I'm asking on behalf of everyone in this courtroom and our families to protect us from this man."

Finally at the end of October 1998, the jury selection process began. If many jurors had tried to get out of jury duty in the 1995 trial, it was nothing compared to the stampede that now ensued. Prospective jurors used every excuse in the book to get out of being selected. To paraphrase a Bette Davis line, they knew that those chosen should "Fasten your seatbelts, it's going to be a bumpy ride."

When the jury trial actually began on November 4, 1998, Benjamin Gonzales remained true to form and refused to wear civilian clothes. He came to court in jail-issue garb. Then he immediately began to disrupt the proceedings. The following exchange gave the jurors just a taste of what they were in for.

Judge Horner: "He [Gonzales] is represented in this matter by his attorney, Mr. Albert Thews."

Thews: "Good morning, ladies and gentlemen. . . ."

Gonzales: "Can I talk to . . ."

Thews: "My client, Mr. Gonzales . . ."

Gonzales: "I'm not your client! You don't come to see me!"

Judge Horner: "Mr. Gonzales, we've had this discussion before. Let him finish addressing the jury and—"

Gonzales: "He just lied."

Judge Horner: "Mr. Gonzales, you have to listen to me. I have things I want to tell the
ladies and gentlemen here. When I'm
through and when they have a chance to
fill out the questionnaire, we can have a
continued discussion on these subjects. I
will do that, Mr. Gonzales."

Finally able to make Gonzales shut up, Deputy D.A. Jacobson and defense attorney Albert
Thews went ahead with the jury selection process.

Then there was an incident so outlandish
that it was only funny in retrospect. Defense
attorney Albert Thews and Deputy D.A. Morris
Jacobson were sitting side by side at the lawyer's table with one empty chair between Benjamin Gonzales and Thews. Thews happened
to glance over at Gonzales and noticed a large
gob of spit hanging down from Gonzales's
mouth. Thews was well aware that Gonzales
had AIDS and how he had spit on his previous
lawyer Les Chettle. Without warning, Thews
suddenly jumped up from his chair and started
running for the door. Jacobson was stunned
for a moment until he too caught a glimpse
of Gonzales, and bolted out of his seat right
behind Thews.

The prospective jurors sat in stunned disbe-
lief at the antics of the two counselors, unable
to understand what was going on. It wasn't until all the commotion had died down that
Thews laughed and told Jacobson, "Sorry, I

would have warned you. But Gonzales was about to spit a big lugee on me and my first reaction was to run."

At least, after Gonzales's initial interruptions, the jury selection proceeded without too many speed bumps. Any one of the prospective jurors could see that this suspect was different from anyone else they had ever seen. By this time he looked like a version of Charles Manson, Jr., with his long hair and unkempt beard. He might occasionally babble to himself or cause minor interruptions, but he was on relatively good behavior, considering some of his other outbursts.

But Gonzales was just biding his time. His most daring assault was slated for the very next day. By the time he was through, no one would have any doubts about just how dangerous he was.

IV

The Most Dangerous Inmate

Twelve

"I'll cut your throat!"

November 5, 1998, started out as just another mildly disruptive day by Benjamin Gonzales in court. He refused once again to wear civilian clothes and was garbed in a red prison jumpsuit. Most of the morning was spent in legal maneuvers by both sides, and the court day ended fairly early. All parties must have heaved a sigh of relief when by the end of the session Benjamin Gonzales had not caused any major outbreaks. But if they did, they were in for a very rude surprise.

Benjamin Gonzales was waiting in the holding area at the court with other prisoners for their ride back to the North County Jail in Oakland. Sheriff's Deputy W. Borland saw everything that happened next and remembered it well. He said, "I was driving van KO3T, a Ford Econoline F-350, fourteen-passenger prison van. It was configured with three custodial compartments. Two side compartments hold five prisoners, and a bench seat behind the driver holds four prisoners. I arrived at the

Superior Court at 1410 and began loading the
van. I loaded two unrestrained female passengers, then five unrestrained male passengers
into the van. Then finally three restrained
male passengers with leg and waist chains onto
the bench seat. A prisoner, Francis MacArthur,
entered first with a boxful of papers. Then
Benjamin Gonzales. Last was inmate Souza.

"I arrived at the Sixth Street entrance to the
North County Jail at about 1420. While waiting
at the gate I heard Gonzales say, 'Stop playing
with me, or I'll cut your throat!'

"MacArthur replied, 'Fuck you!' "

Within moments all hell broke loose. Gonzales lunged at MacArthur, who had his hands
full with the box of papers. Gonzales threw his
waist chain over MacArthur's neck and used it
to hold him down. He kneeled on the fallen
box, using it as leverage to pin MacArthur to
the floor. Gonzales then put a razor blade in
his mouth and began slashing at MacArthur's
throat and face, even though he wore handcuffs. Officer Borland could see blood spatter-
ing on the box. MacArthur's entire face was
becoming a mass of bleeding wounds. The van
was a bedlam of yelling prisoners, the enraged
Gonzales and the helpless MacArthur.

Even though Borland was armed, he did not
enter the van. He played it by the rules, radio-
ing for backup within the North County Jail,
and driving through the gate. The last thing
he wanted was to be overpowered by a van full
of prisoners and suddenly having a loaded gun
loose in the van.

When Borland got the van into the courtyard, he was assisted by Deputies McCann and Nyberg. They opened the side door to find Gonzales leaning over MacArthur, trying to bite him and infect him with AIDS. MacArthur was unconscious and extremely bloody. The whole van was a zoo of yelling prisoners, with a blood-soaked floor.

Finally restraining Gonzales, and hauling him out, Officer McCann heard Gonzales yell, "He just keeps getting inside my head! He needs to stay out of my head!"

Gonzales was led away to the holding tank in H block, while Francis MacArthur was escorted out of the van. He was in complete shock and looked as though he had been mauled by a lion. For the third time in half a dozen years, Benjamin Gonzales sent another person to Highland Hospital as a bloody mess.

Inspector Kathy Boyovich had been on the two-way radio with the van when the whole melee broke out. She heard all the yelling and started yelling herself to the others in the room, "My God, it's Ben! It's Ben! He's at it again!"

The reaction from Judge Jeffrey Horner was swift and draconian. He sent down a court order that was more restrictive than anyone present could remember.

1. The cell and any cell around him [Gonzales] in North County Jail to be searched every day.
2. The defendant to be issued a new set of jail clothing, every day.

3. Gonzales cannot wear multiple layers of clothing.

4. Gonzales to be strip-searched every day.

5. Gonzales to be transported from North County Jail alone.

6. Gonzales to be in his own cell in the courthouse at 1225 Fallon Street, every day.

7. The stairwell from holding cell on 8th floor to court on 7th floor to be searched every day.

8. Gonzales cannot carry folders, paper or parcels with him.

9. If Gonzales wants to pass material to Albert Thews—he has to give it to bailiff first.

10. There are to be three bailiffs present whenever Gonzales [is] there.

11. A. Gonzales is to be transported with waist and ankle chains.

   B. Waist chains are to be modified so Gonzales cannot move hands more than two inches.

   C. While in court, Gonzales's waist chain must be secured to a chair.

   D. While in court, leg chains are to be secured to floor.

   E. Sheriff's bailiff shall have available a special device—a "spit shield"—and the court will decide when to place it on him [Gonzales].

12. Jurors can not pass behind Gonzales, or use the stairwell he uses.

13. No person can approach Gonzales, the water cooler, or coffee machine.

Of all the security measures, the "spit shield" was the most incredible. It looked like the mesh netting worn on a beekeeper's hat, and its purpose was to keep Gonzales from spitting his AIDS-infected saliva on anyone. With his red prison jumpsuit, handcuffs, waist chains, floor chains and spit guard, Benjamin Gonzales looked like a monster sitting at the defense table.

Los Angeles Police Detective Frank Bolan, who had been called up from L.A. to testify about the Dondi Johnson murder, took one look at Gonzales in the courtroom and thought, "My God, he looks just like Hannibal Lecter! This whole courtroom is a scene right out of *Silence of the Lambs.*"

Inspector Kathy Boyovich was also amazed by all the precautions. She said, "He was being treated like a death penalty inmate. They called in security-measure experts to scan the whole area of the jail that he would be in. And even then it was impossible to keep potential weapons out of his hands. The other inmates would leave small chunks of metal or other implements that he could use, hidden in crevices and crannies of the jail."

She thought there were two reasons the other inmates did this. One was that they enjoyed watching Gonzales create some new outrage. It made for an interesting show. The other was that a few were afraid of him and wanted him to go too far. They hoped he would eventually attack some officer and the guard would shoot him.

"There were some inmates there who really hated him and were afraid of him," she said. "They would have liked nothing better than for Gonzales to end up dead. While he was alive, he was not only a threat to those in the courtroom, but to them as well."

That Gonzales was far from being subdued and contrite after the van incident, Kathy Boyovich found out firsthand. She went to photograph the slight wounds Gonzales had received in the attack on Francis MacArthur. When he saw her camera, he went absolutely nuts.

"He went off on me and the guards had to restrain him," she said. "He definitely did not like having his photograph taken."

The trial did not resume after the North County Jail prison van fiasco until November 10. And then there was still a matter of picking the jury. On that date, Deputy D.A. Jacobson excused twenty-three prospective jurors, and defense attorney Albert Thews excused twenty-four. As usual, Gonzales refused to dress in civilian clothes for the trial, and was written up. Judge Horner absolutely banned all media cameras in the courtroom, either film or still cameras. The last thing he needed was to have Gonzales go berserk when the journalists started snapping his photo.

Thews was still getting no cooperation from Gonzales. He sent an aide to talk to Gonzales in his jail cell on November 13, but Gonzales got angry and yelled, "Why doesn't my attorney come!"

When the aide tried to explain that he was representing Thews, the session was over.

The jail personnel led Gonzales away, and one of them said, "Man, you're stupid."

Strangely enough, Gonzales agreed to talk to a *San Francisco Chronicle* reporter named Patricia Jacobus at the North County Jail. "I'm not crazy. I just hear spirits," he told her, and pulled a wad of paper from each ear. "That's why I wear earplugs."

Then he claimed to have multiple personalities—Benny, the charmer, and Pete, the torturer. "Everybody likes Benny," he said. But about Pete he replied, "I could tell you things that would make your hair stand up on end."

Finally on November 17, both the prosecutor and defense attorney were ready to begin their opening statements. But Gonzales was not there to be part of the show. Despite Judge Horner's incredible security measures, Gonzales had still managed to steal a pencil and stab himself in the stomach. And he used a metal clasp to scratch his throat. It got him a trip back to Highland Hospital once again, which is exactly what he wanted. He still dreamed of getting to a phone and calling Nurse Sandi Nakamura. She absolutely filled his thoughts, even in the midst of his trial.

Alameda County Sheriff's Department spokesman, Sergeant Jim Knudsen, told a *San Francisco Chronicle* reporter, "Prisoners have a lot of time to think about how they're going to use things as weapons. Jail is a dangerous place. But the county's jails are safer than they used to be. Now we have twenty-four-hour surveillance with the cameras. Before, we would close the cell doors, then when we opened them, we would find all kinds of stuff."

Because of the latest incident, the judge ordered a guard to always be present and watch Gonzales twenty-four hours a day.

Despite Gonzales's no-show, Deputy District Attorney Morris Jacobson got the ball rolling at 10:20 A.M. on November 17 by telling the jury, "Mr. Gonzales is a creature of habit. He fixates, he deliberates, he premeditates, and he mutilates. He is a methodical, ruthless murderer who killed a card club employee in Los Angeles in 1989, and a strip club dancer in New York City in 1991, the same way he killed Barbara Muszalski at Dave Williams's ranch near Livermore on April 9, 1992." He admitted much of the evidence in the Muszalski killing was circumstantial, but said that he had sufficient evidence to convict.

Jacobson said, "Gonzales confessed to an AIDS counselor that he was obsessed with Muszalski. A Lupin Way mail carrier said Muszalski's pickup was parked blocking the ranch entrance the day of her killing, something she had never seen in her years on that rural route. And when normally punctual [Barbara] Muszalski didn't come home to milk her goats that day, her husband, Jim Muszalski, suspected Gonzales must have been involved somehow. In each case, Gonzales romantically fixates upon, and was rejected by a woman he met while working. In each case, he got the woman alone in a semi-

public place and stabbed her repeatedly in the
face, neck and torso. In each case, he caused a
diversion and fled after the attack."

Deputy D.A. Jacobson's opening statement
lasted for an hour and a half. Defense attorney
Albert Thews was much more brief. His opening statement lasted a total of thirteen minutes.
He stressed that Benjamin Gonzales had not
been charged in either the Los Angeles or New
York slayings and that Jacobson's evidence in
all three cases was either circumstantial or
hearsay.

The opening day of the jury trial ended with
testimony about the New York slaying of
Yvonne Hausley. First on the stand was Steven
Conroy, a co-worker of Gonzales's at the Show
World Theater on 42nd Street back in 1991.
He had known Gonzales at the time as Tony
Perillo. He said from the stand, "Tony killed
her [Yvonne Hausley] in an unused barroom
at the club. It was sort of like the movie *Fatal
Attraction,* except that the man was after the
woman." Then he went on to tell how Gonzales had lured Yvonne into the unused lounge
where they couldn't be seen by anyone.

This first witness also brought the first of
many objections by Thews to the trial. He knew
he had a difficult case, as well as a difficult
client on his hands. But he wasn't going down
without a fight. Deputy D.A. Morris Jacobson
was asking Steven Conroy about what Yvonne
Hausley had told Gonzales at the Show World
Theater concerning her relationship with a policeman. He asked Conroy, "Did you ever hear

her tell him about any other relationship she had?"

Thews immediately shot back, "Calls for hearsay at the time, Judge."

This brought on a legal debate with the jury out of the courtroom. Its scope became indicative of just how these legal questions would go throughout the trial.

Albert Thews argued that whatever Conroy related now that Yvonne Hausley had supposedly said in 1991 was hearsay. Judge Horner referred to the legal questioning on this and cited Witkins's work on California evidence. The case he took as a precedent involved the murder of an elderly widow by the defendant—her handyman. The prosecution in that incident had the nextdoor neighbor of the victim testify that the elderly woman never let strangers into her house. This was admissable to show that she was fearful of strangers, relevant to the theory that the murderer was not a complete stranger to her as the defense attorney contested. Judge Horner said, "So, the instruction I will give is this, if found to be true, you [the jury] may not consider this evidence for the truth of the matter stated, but only as circumstantial evidence tending to show the defendant, Mr. Gonzales, was pursuing Ms. Hausley, and Ms. Hausley was rejecting his advances."

Back before the jury, D.A. Jacobson had a bumpy road in this line of questioning, pockmarked by continuous objections by Albert Thews. Jacobson asked, "At the time that she told the defendant that she had a boyfriend, did she also tell the defendant to leave her alone?"

This brought the immediate response from Thews, "Objection, hearsay."

All the rest of Steven Conroy's recollection of what Yvonne Hausley told Benjamin Gonzales bumped along with starts and stops, in this manner. Conroy got so flustered that he kept drinking water brought to the stand, just to calm himself down.

There was a break in the proceedings until November 23, when Gonzales was once again well enough behaved to attend the trial. On that date, the matter of the attacks on Darrell Oliver and Les Chettle was addressed. The next day was even more dramatic, with testimony by Jim Muszalski and Dave Williams about the disappearance and death of Barbara Muszalski. But Gonzales was not there to witness their testimony. He was acting up again in a big way.

In fact, on November 30, when his old former housemate on the Williams ranch, Patricia Millard, was on the witness stand, as well as RFD mail carrier Katherine Cleek, and AIDS counselor Ivan Meyer, Gonzales had managed to hurt himself once again. Despite all the incredible precautions by Judge Horner, he was able to rip out the stitches in his stomach area and insert four-inch metal rods into his wounds! Where he got those metal rods was anyone's guess. When it came to these mutilations, he was an absolute jail house Houdini. It got Gonzales exactly what he wanted, yet another trip to Highland Hospital with the possibility of conning someone into letting him use a telephone to call Sandi Nakamura.

Inspector Kathy Boyovich also learned a new and disturbing fact. Gonzales was starting to fixate on an attractive female doctor who had been treating him at Highland Hospital. His self-inflicted wounds took on a double threat—not only was he trying to stalk Sandi Nakamura by phone, he was now starting to have fantasies about the Highland Hospital doctor.

"When I found out about this I immediately told the staff at Highland, 'Get her out of there! Do not let her have any contact with Ben!' "

By this time Judge Horner must have been on the verge of pulling all his hair out. He ordered X rays to be performed at Highland Hospital [minus the female doctor] to determine if Gonzales was able to stand trial once more. He wrote, "*All* [his emphasis] security restraints, including headgear are to remain in full force and effect. The telephone security order is also to remain in full force and effect."

On December 1, 1998, while forensic pathologist Dr. Hermann took the stand and discussed Barbara Muszalski's multiple stab wounds, Benjamin Gonzales was having his own self-inflicted stab wound x-rayed, while indeed appearing like some demented Hannibal Lecter. Dr. David Litvak at Highland Hospital wrote in his report, "The Trauma Service evaluated Mr. Benjamin Gonzales at Highland Hospital on December 1, 1998, to determine whether he had sustained an intraperitoneal injury, which might warrant medical observation and for intervention. After initial evaluation, it was deemed Mr. Gonzales had sustained a stab wound to the abdomen with an object that now resided as a foreign body in his abdomen and high likelihood of injury to his small or large intestine. Therefore, emergency exploratory operation of his abdomen was performed with his consent. This operation revealed an absence of injury to any of his abdominal organs and the presence of two foreign bodies [metal rods] which were removed and handed to representatives of the Alameda County Sheriff's Department. Incidentally, Mr. Gonzales was noted to have a small, open skin wound on the surface of his abdomen. Mr. Gonzales's postoperative hospital course is anticipated to be uneventful with possibility of discharge by 12/2/98 or 12/3/98. He will require minor wound care, but otherwise we do not recommend any changes in Mr. Gonzales's treatment or custody status."

Gonzales was not in court on December 2 to hear testimony of crime lab experts Raquel Craft or Sharon Binkley-Smith, tying him to Barbara Muszalski's murder. In some ways their testimony was the most damaging yet. It wasn't just circumstantial. They had discovered his fingerprints in blood, not only on her Chevy S-10 tailgate, but on a business card as well. It would have been extremely difficult for him to leave bloody fingerprints in those locations, and not been present at her murder.

Gonzales made a brief appearance in the courtroom on December 3, but he acted up again and was a no-show on the fourth, while Alameda County Sheriff's Sergeant Brian Lerche spent a day of extensive testimony about the case. In point of fact, Benjamin Gonzales was only getting warmed up and saving his most outrageous behavior for last. Against all attempts by his defense lawyer to keep him off the stand, Gonzales refused to listen to his counselor. He was determined to take the stand on his own behalf. When he was through, even his defense lawyer would be stunned nearly speechless.

Thirteen

"We, the jury . . ."

Even before Benjamin Pedro Gonzales officially took the stand at eleven A.M. on December 8, 1998, there was an incredible exchange between him and Judge Jeffrey Horner. Irritated by the constant wearing of the waist chain, handcuffs and leg chains, Gonzales asked the judge, "Can you loosen these things? I can't take them anymore."

Judge Horner: "Mr. Gonzales, please be quiet. We talked about this before. I'll accommodate you during recess."

Gonzales: "I can't take the pain anymore. My hand's asleep. My feet are asleep."

Judge Horner: "Mr. Gonzales, we've adjusted those three times."

Gonzales: "You adjusted one time."

Judge Horner: "Mr. Gonzales, if you continue, I'll have you removed from the courtroom."

He then cleared the court of jurors.

Gonzales: "That's not my attorney [pointing at Albert Thews]. He never comes to see me. I want to go to sleep. I don't want to come here anymore. Please! This deputy told me he only has dick for me. When I ask, he doesn't have no sugar, that he only has a hard dick for me. He slammed me up against the wall two times yesterday."

Judge Horner: "Mr. Gonzales. Please be quiet. You're not helping your cause, sir."

Gonzales: "I just want to go home and go to sleep. That's all I want to . . . I don't care what happens here. Why drag me over here and torture me? The doctor looked at my hands yesterday and saw the bruises and stuff. There's no reason to treat me like this. I'm not doing anything. I'm willing to be quiet. Why does this guy have to make me nervous and everything? I just want to go somewhere. Feel my hands. He's going to try to make we walk with . . . like this. My feet's asleep. My hand's asleep. I just want to get out of here. You can kill me. Do what you want. I want to die anyway, so what's the difference!"

Defense attorney Albert Thews tried immediately to get this startling outburst stricken from the record. After all, Gonzales had spouted off before the jurors were completely out of the courtroom.

Deputy D.A. Morris Jacobson tried equally hard to get it admitted into evidence.

The admissibility arguments were still going

on when the unkempt, rambling and disheveled Benjamin Pedro Gonzales began to testify from his chair at the defense table on December 8. Security measures were such that he did not take the usual place for testimony on the witness stand.

It was an incredible sight to see. He was still shackled and his head was covered with the spit shield. Los Angeles Police Detective Frank Bolan was right when he said, "It looked like a scene right out of *Silence of the Lambs.*"

After stating his full name, Gonzales was asked by Albert Thews about what happened on April 9, 1992, at Dave Williams's ranch between him and Barbara Muszalski.

Gonzales stated, "You got to excuse me, I'm a little bit nervous now because what I'm about to say. If you can bear with me. I'm in a little bit of pain now."

Then he blurted out before a stunned courtroom, "I'm guilty of the murder, and I just don't know how to say it. They said it would just come out of me. And I'd like to state first to the number of people who think I'm crazy, I'm not crazy. I'm not. I'm not incompetent. I'm competent. Sane. I know I look a little bit odd with this getup. I've protested it in different ways that weren't the best ways.

"I've never disputed that I had . . . I have been guilty. In fact, I'm guilty of many more crimes and many more murders than I'm accused of.

"There's nothing anybody could do to me anymore. I will be dead probably within a year's time, accountable to my AIDS, and I'll never be let loose again. So I mean you can let me walk out of the courtroom right now, and I got to go to other different places. By that time, my AIDS will have killed me or have drove me insane. What the doctors have told me, that one day I'll just wake up and be an idiot.

"So the only thing I have left is my own peace of mind, and if you want to call it soul . . . I call it spirit. I want to alleviate my spirit. My soul.

"And I've read several things in the paper. I've heard several different things. For seven years now, everybody's speculated on what happened. Everybody's accused me of different things. I am guilty. I am far more guilty than many of these murders.

"And including this attack of my lawyer, I did stab him, including cutting. . . . I want to tell how it [the murder of Muszalski] happened. And I want to say the whole thing. I'm sorry. I'm not used to this, and I'm a little bit nervous, like I said.

"I just had two major surgeries in two weeks, plus I'm in a great deal of pain. I'm a little bit agitated because I haven't been eating and all of the other things. I'm in a great deal of pain.

"But I want to say this. I need to say this. I need to alleviate myself. I need for the truth to be known. There's nothing nobody could do to me anymore. I'm finished. I am dead, but I can save my soul. I know that much, and I want to do that.

"In fact, I wanted to speak to the FBI and confess to my many, many other things.

"I'm trying to let [you] know my frame of mind and everything else, and I am getting to the murder, and I am going to explain why and what took place and everything.

"I know there will be a lot of happy people in this courtroom.

"I am so competent that I've been involved in organized crime aspects most of my life. I've done several things. This is one of the reasons why this murder took place right here. It's not that she [Barbara Muszalski] was involved in anything or anything like that. Me and Barb became very close friends, and we became involved in a lot of different things.

"And by the way, I'd like to see a lie detector test to everything I'm saying.

"We argued several times, her and I. I've never loved anybody in my life, and I didn't love Barb or anybody else. In that kind of way, I loved only one person [Nurse Sandi Nakamura], but several years later now that I've been incarcerated. She knew about my aspects with the organized crime and other killings and other things I've done for them . . . loan sharking, importing, exporting drugs and whatnot. She found out by listening to me. . . ."

Thews: "Mr. Gonzales, you've taken the witness stand to testify to the incidents which you are on trial for and not other incidents."
Gonzales: "Thews, could you please let me . . . they can't do nothing to my body, you

know and I'll be dead in a year. Let me do this, Thews, please. You know what I'm saying. I want the truth to be known. I'm telling you what occurred and why it took place, and what happened leading up to that morning. The arguments we were having, her and I [Barbara Muszalski]. They said that I was calling her several times because of love or something like that.

"That had nothing to do with it. Why didn't she call the police? Why didn't she call the FBI? Why didn't she call the authorities? Her argument and my argument was when we argued. . . . I had mentioned one time that I would tell Jim, her husband, everything. She was trying to get me to go, and I said, 'Let me have a chance to leave.' She said several times that she would call the FBI and tell them where I was because I was running, not only from the law, I was running from the people in the organized crime.

"I've never been anybody big in organized crime. I've been a small worker. In fact, I've been most of the time . . . how would you say the race . . . it's not like on TV. TV is totally nonexistent. They all share everybody. And I've been one of the workers that do good work, and I've been honest with them, and I do other things that other people don't do. And I get along with people very well.

I know you look at me real skinny now and whatnot. My average weight is 193.

Even for my height—five-six—is small. I've done a lot of work for them people, and Barb knew about it. She heard me talking on the phone when I used to always call the casinos. When she confronted me about it, the things I spoke about on the phone. So her and I got very close. Then she was having problems with her husband on and off, and then she had problems with . . . her adopted son. And the adopted son was Anglo, and he was living with a black girl at the time . . . Anyway, I kept calling her, trying to ask for more time. She kept saying no more time, no more time. I said, the people in the casino are going to give me my own . . . they owe me, and I was putting my neck out because a lot of them wanted to kill me, because I caused them a lot of trouble with the FBI and everybody else looking for me.

"Anyway, Barb's threatening me with that, and we kept arguing back and forth. One morning, when I was doing my chores, she came early that morning and we argued there. She gave me some rolls of quarters to make some phone calls. She took me to the phone. I told people that I wanted my money, people I was speaking to, at least $5,000 minimum. Which is nothing to them."

Then Gonzales totally disputed the police theory of the murder of Barbara Muszalski at the Williams ranch, even though nothing he said matched the evidence.

Gonzales: "I made her go to . . . Nevada. We argued the whole way down there, which I might add, I had a gun on me. I always carry a gun. I thought I might have to run. The FBI might show up at anytime. So I made her go to Nevada with me, especially a woman driving will be less . . . we won't be stopped. Anyway, we went to Nevada. When we got to Nevada, we were still arguing a lot. And me, I was taking a lot of Valium at the time. I was just stressed. I was mad at everybody, especially the people on the phone. I was mad with her. She kept threatening me. We just kept arguing and arguing and arguing.

"And during one of the arguments in Nevada, I had exploded, and when I exploded . . . I have a very bad temper from when my father used to tie me up and beat me and stuff. I would zone out things, like to zone out his . . . punishment or whatever he called it, abuse. He tied me up nineteen days one time.

"You'll look on the side of my stomach . . . where the scars are . . . his scars. I stabbed myself twenty-two times already on the same side. My stomach looks like a road map on one side.

"Anyway, why I exploded. She started yelling and screaming and slapping me and whatnot. I exploded, and the next thing I know, she is dead. And I'm thinking [I've got] to bury her in Nevada.

"And then the things I hear in my head.

I'm not crazy by the way. If you went to India or you went to the Orient or Africa or someplace, they would know what you mean by speaking to spirits. I've spoken to spirits since I've been a little kid. I'm not crazy. I'm not incompetent.

"I know this sounds odd to you, but speaking to spirits helps me alleviate when my dad used to do the things. . . . So some of the [spirits] were saying to bury her, to get away with everything, they would never find her in Nevada. But at the same time . . . I know this sounds strange, but I got along with Barb very well, and I liked her, and in a lot of ways personally. And I did not want to bury her where the family could not find her, and I knew I would be dead in a few years at that time from AIDS anyway, and I thought the people I worked for would kill me eventually.

"So I wanted to bring her back. So I brought her back, but I also had to come back for my AIDS medication and my tuberculosis medication because they just took like a quart of fluid out of my lung.

"When I came back to the ranch, I put her in the back of the truck. Then we went driving around. The next thing I know . . . we ended up at the airport. And after that, I'm not too sure if I wandered around here for a while or what I quite did, but I ended up in Los Angeles. Then I made it back over here. I'm going through a lot of changes right now . . . what I'm hearing in my head and things. I'm feeling . . . and everything else . . . everything combines. How do you say one thing when everything combines? I know you don't want me to hang myself, Thews. You know what I'm saying? There's no way I can hang myself. I want the truth to be known. Please let me say the truth. I wanted to tell the FBI this. I've been trying to give myself up, not only on this, but the FBI . . . I've been contacted by Mike Wax. . . ."

Thews: "Mr. Gonzales, I want to direct your attention to Santa Rita Jail on April 15, 1994. Were you there in jail at that time?"

Gonzales: "I believe so. I've been in jail seven years."

Thews: Okay. Now, did you know an inmate by the name of Darrell Oliver?"

Gonzales: "Yes. We fought for several months through the door. About the Oliver incident, like I said, I'm guilty of all these crimes but that one. I did fight him. I did. I did beat the hell out of him. But I just got over the flu and pneumonia in ten days. A friend of mine, a biker guy, told me to come out because I wouldn't come out of my cell for all those couple of weeks. And I went downstairs to the phone, to use the phone to call my mother. My mother wasn't there, and I tried making it back up the stairs. And when I went back up the stairs, my friend had said you haven't taken a shower in all these weeks. You should take a shower.

"So I went there and started to take a shower. And the next thing I know, Darrell . . . Darrell is standing at the door, looking and smiling at me because he used to always tell the police, 'Just let me at him for a minute. Just let me take one swing at him. Just let me have one minute with me [sic].'

"But I used to box before, and I know how to fight very well. Even though he was larger than I was and I was sick and whatnot, he and I fought. He and I fought for about fifteen minutes. And I ended up beating him pretty bad.

"Some of the deputies there had told me that they let him out, and the technicians or a deputy . . . I think he's a technician. . . . His name is Helen or Holland . . . he told me he let him out. He was a technician, and he let him out because he was from Livermore, and he went on about the crimes I'm accused of.

"Otherwise, they said I fixed my door. If I could have fixed my door, I would have fixed it a lot. I have other enemies, and I would have come out with objects because I can get my hands [on] basically anything I want. I would have come out with a weapon and killed my enemy. I would not have come out and went in a shower naked while he's clothed. I'm innocent of that one.

"I have tried to put a complaint on that. But the deputies I was having problems with were keeping my papers when I filed it in some court or something like that. And by the time I did get my papers, the deputy said it was too late to pursue it.

"But I don't know what else to say about that one. That one I'm innocent on."

Thews: "Mr. Gonzales, directing your attention to Department 8 in this Superior Courthouse, March the sixteenth, 1995—that's Judge Baranco's court—were you represented by attorney Les Chettle at that time?"

Gonzales: "Yes, and I did stab him. I did stab Les Chettle with a pencil, and I hit him one time. Les Chettle and I were fighting all the time because he would not come and see me. I wanted him . . . Basically, the first lawyer I had was a good lawyer, and I wanted that lawyer. I knew some people in South America, and I wanted to be extradited to South America because in South America . . . I could do my time down there if I'm married or have kids down there. And I could do my time down there, and eventually I could pay somebody to get released. And the first lawyer was doing this for me.

"And Les Chettle . . . I was trying to get him to do this for me, and he would not do this for me.

"And the drug people that were at the time helping me, were . . . already to the point where they had a lawyer come down and take pictures of me to send to South

America to fix my paperwork to try to get me extradited to South America.

"I don't know if I would have got to go, but at the time when the cartel . . . the cartel is no more of a cartel, but at that time the cartel was very strong and political.

"And I knew a few people down there, especially with my work and my reputation.

"So I tried to get Les Chettle to cooperate with me in a lot of different ways. He wouldn't even come and listen to my case.

"The day of court, he came upstairs in a room with me when I was unhandcuffed, unchained, everything, and I told him I wanted to do . . . to talk to people in South America, called the same numbers and people that the other lawyer was calling. He would not do it. We argued, and I told him I heard what the judge said because I was in the stairway, and I heard the judge ask the D.A. what made Mr. Gonzales snap after all these years. He seemed to lead a pretty normal life, and all of a sudden he just went on a spree of killing. It was not that I went on a spree of killing.

"But anyway, I wanted that on the record because the judge was speaking to the D.A. about it.

"And the lawyer was so scared of Judge Baranco, he wouldn't do it. We argued about that. And I told him I did not want him for a lawyer.

"And somebody had told me at the

time . . . if I went to a mental hospital, then when I came back, I would be with another lawyer.

"So I asked him if I could go to a hospital, and he and I argued about that too. He said it was too late for all that.

"And then that same day, I didn't do nothing to him in that cell upstairs. I was unhandcuffed and unchained, everything. We were in there alone. By the time the deputies got to us, I could have did whatever I wanted to.

"Then when we came down here, I was still talking to him about that, still trying to convince him about that. I had a long pencil in this hand, about five-inches long, and I had a short pencil in this hand which was about three-and-a-half-inches long which were sharpened on both ends. Now, if I wanted to plan to stick him or do anything to him or even kill him, I could have. I could have gotten many different weapons.

"I just recently stuck two five-inch pieces of steel in me. So I mean I could have got my hands on anything. They caught me with razors, other knives and things.

"I could tell you right now where three knives are in this courthouse.

"Anyway, I asked to speak to Mr. Chettle again because he said he'll talk to me before court. So I wanted to keep him on my project. So we talked in this stairway, and when we talked, he came in. He shut the door, and I was sitting on the steps. I was writing on the tablet. And I was letting him know a little bit more information about South America. I told him if nothing else, at least I want on the record about the judge, what he said to the D.A. and what the D.A. was talking to him about. He was saying no, and he's not going to do it, and he doesn't have to, several things. I wanted to participate in picking a jury and all this other stuff. And we started arguing.

"When I got frustrated and mad, it's like turning a pair of binoculars around, and you start seeing things from tunnel vision, and you start zoning . . . zoning things out, and you are [seeing] a little, little, little less. And people say it's temper, but it's far more than a temper. It's something else.

"So I started hearing the things in my head that he was against me, that he was doing this and that. Then I started hearing some other things from a couple of other characters . . . you want to call them characters. There's some people call them spirits. And the basic violent one is Pete.

"And the next thing I know, the more I tried to push him away, Pete had already stabbed him with a little pencil, not the big pencil, but the little pencil in the chest and socked him one time.

"If Pete wanted to kill him, Pete could have killed him very easily and maimed him pretty bad, stuck him in the eye with the pencil, many different things. We just wanted to show that we didn't want the lawyer.

"I'm very, very capable of killing somebody, and I know how to kill somebody. And I could do it very, very easily.

"And I know how to fight very well. A lot of people are surprised how well I could fight. . . . So I stood over him looking at what happened. And I ran up the first flight of stairs. Then the deputy came in. He looked at him. Then he said, 'Stop.' But I'm already stopped. I figured get away from him, get away from Chettle and they'll just handcuff me.

"Anyway, I was stopped, and I could see that he was in a bad mood because me and that deputy was arguing before because I don't get along with deputies. "Of course, I do get along with many other deputies.

"I ran up the top of the flight of stairs. He said stop. I had nowhere to go because the door was closed. I stopped and sat down on a flight of stairs.

"He said lay on your stomach. I laid on my stomach. He stood on my head. He actually stood on my head. They beat the shit out of me, took turns beating the shit out of me naked.

"I have a witness to that, and I tried to present the witness to what occurred. I have filed paperwork on this.

"The deputies tried to get me to plead

guilty, not only to this crime, but to other crimes that I would not plead guilty to."

Thews: "Mr. Gonzales, the district attorney has introduced evidence of a similar murder in New York, and the district attorney has introduced evidence of a similar murder in Los Angeles. Do you want to talk about those two cases?"

Gonzales: "Yes. I'm going to do this [to] let everybody be happy, especially Jacobs [sic]. Jacobs has been decent to me. I got to say it my way to come out, please. I'm too damn nervous. I got to say it my way. I know you got a way of doing things. I'm trying to cooperate, but let me say it my way. I feel defenseless. I want to do this. I want to do this. I am guilty of both murders. Both girls. Both girls were involved with the same people I was. The people were mad at them. I'm guilty of both murders. Because of those people. You know what I'm saying? Please let me say I'm getting agitated. You know the medication's wearing off. I'm hearing different things in my head. Being agitated toward the man, because I'm trying to do this properly for every . . . I cannot put my head on a platter for everybody and give everybody a piece of me. What else do you want? Let me have a little bit out of this."

Judge Horner: "Mr. Gonzales, Mr. Thews is giving you a chance to describe things pretty much in your words, but you really have to follow his questions about the subject areas, and right now he's asking you to describe the incident in New York or an incident on March 24, 1991, involving Yvonne Hausley."

Gonzales: "Jeff, I was told when I did this I could say what I want to say at first, then everybody question me, chop it up or do whatever they want to do. That's what I was told. You know what I'm saying? If I have to do everybody's way and do it like that, it's not going to mean anything to me, and it's not going to do anything. Everybody knows I'm guilty. I want to say the way I'm guilty. I want the record to be straight because I am not a serial killer. I've killed many people, but I'm not a serial killer. Please, Jeff, let me do this. I'm really, really agitated. I'm hearing things that I don't want to hear in my head. I don't want to zone out of everything. Let me speak my piece and then you can chop me up. I don't care. Jeff, I'm having a very, very, very difficult time because aspects don't want me to say this, and aspects do want me to say this, and I'm fighting within myself to say it. And I need to say it because if I don't say it, then the other aspects are going to win, and I'm not going to say anything, and I do not want to stay in limbo. I do not want to be with my dad when I die."

Thews: "Mr. Gonzales, tell us about Yvonne Hausley in New York, please."

Gonzales: "They were all involved in organized

crime, with the organized crime people I was involved with. They all knew too much about smaller people . . . the smaller people in organized crime who some of the bigger ones got afraid of. A lot of things. It's like when I went . . . God, I'm losing it. I'm hearing you. I'm hearing something in my head. I'm hearing too many things. That's the reason I stabbed myself twenty-two times. To prove a point. To get a point across."

Thews: "Mr. Gonzales, be quiet."

Judge Horner: "Mr. Thews, let me interject. Why don't you ask some directed questions regarding time and location that can direct Mr. Gonzales's specific attention to the facts which have been the subject—"

Gonzales: "Why don't you ask me about L.A.?"

Judge Horner: "Hang on a second. We'll get to Los Angeles in a moment. I'm suggesting to Mr. Thews some questions here."

Thews: "I'll start over, but, Your Honor, I cannot go much farther than a free narrative. I've set the stage. . . . Mr. Gonzales, I want to direct your attention to March 24, 1991, at a place called Show World in New York. At that time, you were known as Tony Perillo. Yvonne Hausley was there at about one o'clock in the afternoon. Tell us what happened with Yvonne."

Gonzales: "You know, Thews, I asked to come from the state hospital down here to do this. They wanted to keep me there for life. I came down here specifically to do that.

I've been trying to fight . . . everybody to
do that. I been stabbing myself not to delay
court. I stabbed myself to get my point
across to the media, to put me on TV, put
me on a lie detector to confess. I want to
admit all this. Let me say that's my fucking
way. . . . Why can't you let me spurt out
everything? To get it out. Then you guys
can put in sections and chop it up, do
whatever you guys want to do with it. We
save time. You don't hear what my
head . . . I don't understand you guys. I'm
fighting with my head. I came from the
state hospital to do this. I am not crazy. I
am not. See, that's the reason I wanted
them to subpoena Sandi. Sandi knows all."

Judge Horner: "Hold on, Mr. Gonzales. Let
me ask you a question, Mr. Gonzales.
You've indicated you want to talk about
Los Angeles."

Gonzales: "Yes, but I want to speak . . . see,
everything is intertwined. You're going
back and forth from Los Angeles to New
York. Many different times I'm doing projects for those people. These were parts of
the projects I was supposed to do. Not
Barb; the other projects I was supposed to
do. I did not want to do them. I refused
to do them. They got mad at me and
threatened me for me to do the project. . . ."

Thews: "Mr. Gonzales, I want to direct your attention to Los Angeles on February the
fourth, 1989, and to a young lady by the

name of Dondi Andrea Johnson. What happened after she left work at the poker club at about 4:58 in the morning of that day?"

Gonzales: "She was involved in drug dealing and drug laundering. I got her involved in a lot of stuff to help pay off the money that she had owed a lot of bosses. She had used to sell crack and was a crack addict. Her and her so-called boyfriend, who she was messing around with two different guys in the house at the same time . . . I was never in love with Dondi. She was prostituting herself at the casino at the same time. I have a problem with it because of the boss at the casino, because for the money she kept stealing and everything else. They wanted her done as a project, but they didn't want to get a lot of people involved in it because she was so low level and she was considered nothing by those people.

"And I was responsible for her because I brought her in. I told her that she could pay off some of the stuff by participating in a project down in New York. But she kept saying that she wanted to be put in a position where she could make a lot of money all the time.

"And I told her that I was not going to stick my neck out for her. She had to talk to several of the casino people.

"See, see, that's why I specifically want Sandi subpoenaed because she knows pieces that I'm missing."

Thews: "Mr. Gonzales, Sandi is not involved in this case."

Gonzales: "She was involved with this case, and she tried to hide this."

Thews: "Mr. Gonzales, Sandi has not been involved in this case under the district attorney's view of the case."

Gonzales: "She tried to hide these murders with me. How is she not involved? I'm on one of her phone bills."

Judge Horner: "Mr. Gonzales, let me talk for a moment. We've had hearings involving that issue, and I've indicated that that's not part of this case."

Gonzales: "That's what I'm trying to focus on. And not only that, they're trying to make me out as a stalker or something like that. Even the chaplain . . . she even talked to the chaplain about coming down here to see me. I got her letters. Please read her letters. See, Sandi knows . . ."

Judge Horner: "Hang on, Mr. Gonzales. Let's take a break now for noon."

After a noon break, Benjamin Gonzales was right back on the stand pleading to see Sandi Nakamura once more. In fact, his whole admission of guilt was a grandstand play to catch a glimpse of Sandi Nakamura in court. If he wasn't a stalker, nothing he said now was likely to disprove that notion. He was absolutely frantic to see Sandi. Even though his defense attorney tried to get him back to the murders of Yvonne Hausley in New York, and Dondi Johnson in Los Angeles, he became adamant in his quest to have Sandi Nakamura present.

Gonzales: "I'd like to state to the jurors when you read my testimony and other testimony, the transcripts, please read my AIDS counselor's testimony where she testified that she used to call and talk to the woman, Sandi Nakamura. I say this quickly before I do the other answers because I feel real bad that my own lawyer would indicate that I'm a stalker and serial killer.

"The reason is, Sandi has a crypt for me, a crypt for her, the same coffins, same place. She's divorced her husband at the time. She was hiding me in the state hospital. She was fixing my records. She was on the voting team to keep me at the hospital or bring me back here. I was going to stay at the hospital with her continuously, but I've been back here. We had plans to get married. She bought me a wedding ring and was getting prepared to come down here with me. I have all of the letters.

"My AIDS counselor knows about this. The chaplain knows about that, which nobody has called for witnesses. As soon as they start speaking about it, nobody wants to hear it. My lawyer mentioned to me about six months ago when I asked if Sandi is going to be subpoenaed, he said no . . . the district attorney does not want

her down here, nor does the court. I asked
the investigator later on, and said the same
thing.

"Me and her have been fighting for
some time now about this thing. She's
afraid of this because her and I have done
many crimes together and conspiracy. She
is even buying a gun, so I could get out
of the hospital at one point. I have records
of all this. And the reason I'm inculpating
[sic] her, is not to hurt her. I'll do anything
because they'll never, ever hurt Sandi, because Sandi knows too much about me. As
soon as she gives the information about
me, they just leave her alone. I want to set-
tle this with Sandi. . . . Sandi is more the
schizophrenic type girl. She's a very nervous girl. She's ten years older than I am.
She had a problem with her family. And
then she went and married . . . she's Anglo, and she went and married a Japanese
fellow. She's been in like captivity for
twenty-five years. I was the first person she
met out of her life. The only friend she
has. She has nobody. She has no one.

"I wanted her to come because I wanted
somebody to know everything I ever did in
my life, because the doctors said I was finally
going to turn into an idiot. She accepted
everything I explained to her. Details on everything. She even knows where the murder
weapons are. The parts I'm missing in my
head, she knows about. I ask for her to be
subpoenaed here. I am not stalking Sandi.

Sandi has a birthmark on her crotch area about as big as a silver dollar and again on her back. I would not know those birthmarks unless I've seen her naked. She cannot deny anything because if you let me bring in proof tomorrow, I'll bring in proof in her own writing.

"Sandi was trying to help me escape [when] I was at the hospital. She was buying a gun. They knew that we were messing around together because we kept disappearing in linen closets, and the nurse's office and other places.

"Sandi knows the different aspects of me. She knows that I could go into different people inside my head which are spirits. I am not crazy.

"I am not incompetent.

"I want the truth to be known. All the newspapers and everybody speculate on everything. I won't take a picture because I'm tired of fighting everybody in jail. Them saying I'm a rapist and this and that.

"I've never been accused of a sexual crime. I'm not a rapist or a child molester or something like that.

"And I've also been on *America's Most Wanted* and a number of other programs. As soon as I'm on TV, I have a problem right away. I do not want no more problems. As many people as I've hurt, I'm capable of hurting others. If you subpoena Sandi, I will give you at least a minimum of ten murders. I will not go into a few others because I do still have family, and I'm not going to implicate some of the people that are involved in those. Some people that stepped out of the so-called line of business, and do have families now and children and stuff. I'm not going to disrupt their lives.

"But I will give you enough to show you that I'm not a serial killer. I do not have nothing against women. I have killed more men than women. . . . If it was like the newspapers said and everything else, I could be living out this very good life with plenty of money. I could get any identification I want anytime I want. They could never catch me.

"The only reason they even caught me now is because I've let myself get caught because of the things I've heard in my head. . . .The person who picked up the papers with me in Mexico . . . his family has connections. They are in law enforcement and the government in Mexico. We came back over here to California where I could pick up at least $5,000 minimum overnight from one of my enemies, but I figured he was not going to betray me because I betrayed a friend of his and cost him like $200,000 in the loan sharking business. Anyway, so when I called him, he betrayed me to get even for his friend.

"My father's put me through a great deal of trauma. I'm going to cope with what little bit of life I got left.

"I don't know what else to say. I'm not a serial killer, and I'm not a stalker. I'm not stalking Sandi. I'm hoping after everything is through with the courts and everything, me and her could come to an understanding, even if it's just friends. We're going to be buried in the same place either way. She's already got the crypts. She's already got the coffins together. We got the rings."

Finally Judge Horner had enough of his rambling and transparent attempts to get Sandi Nakamura into court. He tried to steer Gonzales back to the New York murder, but Benjamin would not be swayed. He kept calling The Honorable Jeffrey Horner "Jeff," and pleading with him to subpoena Sandi. He swore that she was the only person who "knows everything." He complained that his memory was now faulty, but that Sandi would help him clear it up.

Albert Thews kept trying to lead Gonzales along, but Ben's response to him was, "Thews, you're [acting] like I'm doing something outrageous or something. You know, I feel stunned. You get Sandi down here . . . and she'll save her own butt."

By this point, Thews had also had enough with his client, and turned him over for re-direct by Deputy D.A. Morris Jacobson.

Morris Jacobson was fuming after Benjamin

Gonzales's soliloquies defaming the names of the women he had stalked and murdered. He was not going to let Gonzales slide off into long tirades. It would be more like a game of tennis now, with the ball being hit back and forth across the net by these two.

Jacobson: "Mr. Gonzales, you see this exhibit one?"

Gonzales: "Yes."

Jacobson: "You see those pictures of the three women here?"

Gonzales: "Yes."

Jacobson: "Who is the middle one?"

Gonzales: "Barb."

Jacobson: "Who is the one over here on the right, labeled A?"

Gonzales: "I'm not too sure. I'd have to guess that was . . . Dondi, but it don't look nothing like her, not the one I know."

Jacobson: "How about the C photo? Is that Yvonne Hausley?"

Gonzales: "I would have to guess so, but it don't look like her either. . . . But what is the problem? I already admitted to killing them, everybody."

Jacobson: "You know Mr. Gonzales, I got a couple of questions for you though."

Gonzales: "I know you very well, Jacobs [sic]. I know where you're upset. And I know you're upset with me."

Jacobson: "I want to ask you some things about what happened between you and Barb Muszalski. Okay?"

Gonzales: "Okay."

Jacobson: "What did you kill her with?"

Gonzales: "A knife."

Jacobson: "Where did you get the knife?"

Gonzales: "The knife I used to cut the strings of hay."

Jacobson: "Did you take blankets out of Dave Williams's garage and cover the seats in that truck, Mr. Gonzales?"

Gonzales: "I remember covering the seats with something. I can't remember what I covered them with. Everything seems so far . . . when you're going through something, it's like the binoculars turned around. Somebody trying to talk to me. I won't talk, and he yelled in my ear."

Jacobson: "I want to talk to you about the very first stab wound. Where did it land? Was it right in the middle of her chest?"

Gonzales: "I, I, I have no idea where. By the time I'm even conscious, it's already all over. It doesn't happen where you see something. I would have shot her if this was going to be like that. I had a gun on me. I would have shot her if that was going to be like that. A rage killing."

Jacobson: "So you can't tell us which of the twenty-three or twenty-four stab wounds to Barbara's body . . . which was the first one?"

Gonzales: "No. I know it was me, because I was there. I'm the one who killed her."

Jacobson: "How long were you thinking about

killing her before you did it, Mr. Gonzales?"

Gonzales: "I never thought about killing Barb. If I thought about killing Barb, why don't I just shoot her and just go on?"

Jacobson: "Did you think about killing Yvonne Hausley in New York before you killed her?"

Gonzales: "No."

Jacobson: "Never thought about it ahead of time?"

Gonzales: "No."

Jacobson: "Did you think of killing Dondi Johnson ahead of time?"

Gonzales: "No."

Jacobson: "So it just kind of happened, right?"

Gonzales: "My rage is a little bit different."

Jacobson: "What triggered your rage with Barbara, Mr. Gonzales?"

Gonzales: "Tiredness, aggravation from people that owed me money, her always coming at me with the FBI . . . and me yelling back and forth at her. Her husband, this and that. We both agreed he already [knew] and we both agreed that he already knows. . . . And she said she had another affair at the time and that I just be doing something and hurting people because when two couples get angry at each other and they fight, they become enemies and the last time she had an affair with some guy or something—"

Jacobson: "Mr. Gonzales, let me interrupt for a second. This rage you're talking about,

is this the same rage you felt towards
Yvonne Hausley when you killed her?"

Gonzales: "How do you say the same rage? If
you ask Sandi, she'll know everything."

Jacobson: "We'll talk about Sandi in a little
while."

Gonzales: "I'm not an idiot. You're avoiding
her."

Jacobson: "Don't worry, Mr. Gonzales. I'm going to come back to Sandi. But I want to
ask you right now about whether the rage
you felt when you killed Barbara was the
same rage you felt when you killed Yvonne
Hausley?"

Gonzales: "How do you say the same rage? It's
just like when I attacked MacArthur on this
bus. I didn't plan to attack MacArthur. Me
and him had disputed before. It just came
out. By the time I even know it, I had a
razor at his throat, and I just about cut his
jugular vein."

Jacobson: "Mr. Gonzales, can you control your
rages?"

Gonzales: "No."

Jacobson: "When you were beating Darrell
Oliver in the shower, you were able to control your rage that day, weren't you?"

Gonzales: "No."

Jacobson: "As soon as the deputy told you to
stop, you stopped, didn't you?"

Gonzales: "No. I was already stopped, and I
was already climbing out of the shower,
and the deputies were walking down from
the long part of the hall, and I was going

into my room, which was right there, like two inches away, and the door was open."

Jacobson: "Mr. Gonzales, let me ask you another question. When you stabbed your attorney in Department 8 behind a door just like that . . . you stopped as soon as the door opened and the deputy came in. Isn't that right?"

Gonzales: "I could have killed Mr. Chettle. I could have shoved the pencil in his eye. I could have knocked the hell out of him. He would have at least had a broken nose, broken something in his face. I could have seriously damaged him a great deal. And in those days I weighed a great deal more, and I used to exercise all the time. I used to work out with 305 pounds . . . I wouldn't say I stopped myself. It's not me that stopped. It was probably Bennie."

Jacobson: "Oh, this is your thing about having multiple personalities, right?"

Gonzales: "No, I don't have multiple personalities."

Jacobson: "Bennie, the nice guy, and Pete, the mean guy."

Gonzales: "No, it's not quite like that."

Jacobson: "Did you say it was Pete that attacked Mr. Chettle?"

Gonzales: "He was angry with him."

Jacobson:"Let's talk mental condition a little bit, Mr. Gonzales. . . . It wasn't that you wanted to leave the state hospital. It's that they wouldn't keep you—you weren't sick. Isn't that right, Mr. Gonzales?"

Gonzales: "No. I came here to get married to Sandi. That's more important to me than anything in the world."

Jacobson: "Mr. Gonzales, I want you to listen to my question, tell me whether you heard this before: 'Mr. Gonzales's clinical presentation is consistent with the intentional production of false or grossly exaggerated symptoms of cognitive impairment.' "

Gonzales: "No."

Jacobson: "Do you remember them kicking you out of there because they found you faking your symptoms?"

Gonzales: "Faking my symptoms? No."

Jacobson: "Do you remember telling a psychologist up here in Alameda County that you couldn't read, write, or spell, and the folks at Patton State Hospital caught you writing letters to the nurse there, Sandi Nakamura?"

Gonzales: "They didn't catch me right out with Sandi. They caught some notes. They weren't too sure who it was to because Sandi's name wasn't on it. Yeah, we were passing notes, and my spelling is not too great."

Jacobson: "In the letter that they intercepted, you use the words 'manipulate,' 'drugs,' 'agony,' 'pleasure,' 'imagine,' 'classification,' 'especially,' 'emotions,' and 'frustration.' Did you spell all of those words correctly and use them in proper context in your letter?"

Gonzales: "I don't know. I always have a dic-

tionary. I know how to use a dictionary. . . .
I'm a little mixed up here because I confessed to everything and now you're prose-
cuting me like I'm trying . . . like I'm
lying. I admitted to everything. What more
do you want?"

Jacobson: "Mr. Gonzales, I still want to talk to
you about your mental state. You seem to
be suggesting to this jury that you're hearing voices in your head and having a conflict. I wanted to ask you about that."

Gonzales: "I am not crazy. I do not hear voices
like a crazy person. They're not voices.
They're spirits. If you went to the Orient
or India or a reservation or something,
they would know what I'm talking about."

Jacobson: "Mr. Gonzales, you spent plenty of
time faking being crazy though, didn't
you?"

Gonzales: "No, I have not. . . . I have only
one year to live. . . . If you send me back
right now, I'll get on TV and say a whole
bunch of different things once I get to the
hospital. They put me on medication from
A to Z. I am not going to spend the last
year of my life zoned out on medication.
Especially with the record I'm doing, stab
myself twenty-two times, cut my throat,
swallowed a razor and all the other stuff."

Jacobson: "Mr. Gonzales, you referred to the
judge here in the courtroom today as 'Jeff'
several times, by his first name, correct?"

Gonzales: "Yes."

Jacobson: "All right. Do you remember during

that competency trial, do you remember what you called him then? Did you call him 'the overseer' and 'the overseeing in the stone chair'?"

Gonzales: "No, I compared him to the overseer. He sits there overseeing in that chair."

Jacobson: "This whole business of Bennie, the nice guy, and Pete, the mean one, is something you just came up with in the last couple of weeks?"

Gonzales: "Bennie is not the nice guy. Bennie can kill somebody. Bennie is the referee."

Jacobson: "Mr. Gonzales, let's get back to talking about the murders. You said Sandi knows where the murder weapons are, right?"

Gonzales: "Yes. . . . Then you won't bring Sandi down here? I'm trying to close this whole book. You're trying to close a page or chapter. For some reason, you don't want to bring Sandi down. . . . In fact, you're agitating me real bad, especially when I don't have no more medication in me."

Jacobson: "What will you do, cut me, Mr. Gonzales?"

Gonzales: "No, but I could protest in lot of other different ways. You know what I'm saying? I don't need to hurt you physically. I am not a stupid person. I am not crazy. . . . If you want to know anything else, you ask Sandi. . . . I can't believe it.

I even told you how it went down. I even said other things. I mean, my God."

Jacobson: "Mr. Gonzales, have you spent any time reading the law . . . about voluntary manslaughter?"

Gonzales: "No."

Jacobson: "Is it something you've been studying up on?"

Gonzales: "No. I draw and write my frustrations out."

Jacobson: "You ever heard of the concept of heat of passion?"

Gonzales: "No."

Jacobson: "You ever heard of the concept of provocation?"

Gonzales: "I don't even know what the word is."

Jacobson: "You had some idea in your head before you came into the courtroom today to testify that you needed to tell the jury something about how you and Barbara had some kind of fight. That way you could reduce your responsibility for her killing. . . . So does Sandi Nakamura know what you said to Barbara Muszalski to get her to come over that day?"

Gonzales: "You just asked me that question. I told you I did not say anything to get her over there. And . . . you're making a mockery for some reason. . . . I'm not quite sure why you want to do that. I thought you would be more happier than everybody else. I hear the anger and frustration in you. I thought it would be coming from him [pointing at defense attorney Albert Thews]. He's the one who disputes me all the way."

Jacobson: "Mr. Gonzales, did you kill Barbara Muszalski in front of Dave Williams's house?"

Gonzales: "No."

Jacobson: "Where did you kill her?"

Gonzales: "In Nevada."

Jacobson: "Where in Nevada?"

Gonzales: "After the phone call."

Jacobson: "Did you kill her while the truck was moving?"

Gonzales: "No."

Jacobson: "While it was stopped?"

Gonzales: "Yeah . . . why don't you ask Sandi about it? I killed Barbara. What is the big thing? I know it. Everybody else knows it. I confessed to it. I feel dirty now. I thought I was feeling a little bit relieved, you know. And I feel dirty. I thought I was going to have to come down and fight with this guy [defense attorney Thews]. I did not know I have to come back and fight with you. I thought you were going to help defend me in here. I mean I felt the aggression from you. I'm not sure why. I thought you would be the happiest person in the world."

Jacobson: "Mr. Gonzales, you sure have cleared up any concept that you weren't the one that did it. That part is clear. But you're telling us that you're hearing all these voices, you were on Valium that day, you don't remember, and ask Sandi, right?

You had a rage. Am I missing one of the excuses?"

Gonzales: "I did the murder. What more do you want?"

Jacobson: "Did you commit a first-degree murder, Mr. Gonzales, with premeditation and deliberation?"

Gonzales: "Premeditation is beforehand?"

Jacobson: "Yeah, thinking about it ahead of time."

Gonzales: "Do you think I'm stupid to do something so sloppy and let everybody know or something? I've done murder you couldn't even find a clue to. I'm not a sloppy person. I'm not stupid."

Jacobson: "Right. One of the things you do is systematically destroy evidence after a crime. Like with Dondi Johnson, you set the car on fire, burned all the evidence."

Gonzales: "Now you're playing a game with me. I told you to ask Sandi. You're going to play a game with me. You will not. You want to ask me anything more, subpoena Sandi. I am not going to play your game. For some reason I thought you'd be happy. . . . I am not stupid. Nobody would have even found her. I mean I could have used gloves. I could have used different places. I could have used somebody else. . . . The way she was killed. You could see that it was in a rage."

Jacobson: "So it's just a rage, accidental kind of thing, right?"

Gonzales: "It's not an accidental thing. A rage is a rage. How can a rage be accidental?"

Jacobson: "Why did you stab her in the eyes?"

Gonzales: "Huh?"

Jacobson: "Why did you stab her in the left eye?"

Gonzales: "I don't know."

Jacobson: "You were there, weren't you?"

Gonzales: "I mean I don't know what to say at those times. It was a rage."

Jacobson: "How do you explain a rage?"

Gonzales: "My God, what do you want me to say to that . . . ? It's strange. Like right now I'm so far back in my head to not answer you, and at the same time I'm frustrating, and at the same time part of me wants to say something to you."

Jacobson: "Let's talk about inmate MacArthur. Remember when you were attacking him with a razor, did you stop yourself, or did the deputy tell you to knock it off, to stop?"

Gonzales: "It was like when I zoned back, I already had the razor to his throat, and I was going to cut, and I said, 'What the hell am I doing?' I was like trying to come back, you know. I didn't want to cut the man, you know. I didn't hear nothing about kill him, kill him, kill him."

Jacobson: "Let's talk about Dondi Johnson for a minute. Do you remember what you told us before lunch, that she was prostituting herself, that was one of the things said, right?"

Gonzales: "She was in the casino prostituting herself. Also she was a crack dealer and a few other things too. We won't get into that. Evidently you're trying to make some kind of fool out of me."

Jacobson: "Mr. Gonzales, this whole business about Dondi Johnson being a crack dealer and prostitute . . . you're lying to this jury about that, aren't you . . . ? Isn't it a fact that she was a twenty-two-year-old young woman who was a full-time college student at the time?"

Gonzales: "That's not true."

Jacobson: "Isn't it a fact that she was working part-time at night to finance her education?"

Gonzales: "It's not true."

Jacobson: "Isn't it a fact, Mr. Gonzales, that one week before you cut her to pieces and burned her body that she was elected to the student senate at Cerritos Junior College?"

Gonzales: "I don't know nothing about that. . . . You're making a mockery [out of this]. For some reason I feel alleviated, and now I feel dirty somehow, and I can't figure out how. And I can't figure out why you're doing this."

Jacobson: "Mr. Gonzales, I'm showing you exhibit two—"

Gonzales: "You ain't showing me nothing, because I ain't participating in this anymore."

Jacobson: "You willing to look at photos, Mr. Gonzales?"

Gonzales: "No."

Jacobson: "Do you want to look at the photos of Barbara Muszalski?"

Gonzales: "I'm not going to look at no photos."

Jacobson: "Why not, Mr. Gonzales?"

Gonzales: "Because I'm not an animal. . . . You're not messing my head up. It's messed up enough already. . . . You ask Sandi. Sandi knows the real me."

Jacobson: "She knew you were H.I.V. positive, didn't she?"

Gonzales: "Yes. She was my nurse there."

Jacobson: "But you were telling us that you and her been getting it on in the linen closet down there, right?"

Gonzales: "In the nurse's office, too, and the . . . room, like where they vote."

Jacobson: "Are you willing to answer questions about the murder of Barbara Muszalski?"

Gonzales: "I told you ask Sandi about any of that stuff."

Jacobson: "Are you going to ask Sandi as to every one of these questions on Barbara Muszalski?"

Gonzales: "Probably so. That's what I'm hearing in my head. . . . [Turning to the Judge.] Jeff, with all due respect, what are you going to do, put me on death row? It's to alleviate this. I killed all these people, so . . ."

Jacobson: "Did you meet Sandi after you killed
    Dondi Johnson in L.A.?"
Gonzales: "Ask her."
Jacobson: "Be a man. Answer the question, Mr.
    Gonzales."
Gonzales: "You be a man. Ask Sandi."
Judge Horner: "Please answer the question,
    Mr. Gonzales."
Gonzales: "He's not going to make it ugly,
    Judge. I don't care [what] the price is. I'm
    not going back to my room and feel
    dirty. . . . I'm surprised, Jacob [sic]. I felt
    of all the people you would be happy and
    everything else. I'm really surprised, and
    I'm sure someday I'll figure out what
    you're doing."

From this point on, Benjamin Gonzales absolutely refused to answer any more questions.
He sat as still as a rock beneath his spitting
device and spoke not a word in response to
the deputy district attorney's questions.

The questions were pointed and telling coming from Morris Jacobson. "Mr. Gonzales, you
told us that you knew where there are three
knives in the courthouse here. You also told us
that you didn't want anyone else to get hurt
anymore. Would you tell us, please, where
those knives are so we can avoid further inju-
ries to other prisoners or civilians in the courthouse?"

Silence.

"Mr. Gonzales, you say you want to be at
peace with yourself and alleviate your spirit.

Why is it then you continue to attack the character of the three women who you so brutally murdered?"

Silence.

"Isn't it a fact, Mr. Gonzales, that you still want to hurt these three women because each of them rejected you?"

Silence.

"Mr. Gonzales, you told us you killed at least ten people. How many people have you killed?"

Absolute silence.

All the questions were done now. It was up to defense attorney Albert Thews to try to extricate Benjamin Gonzales from the very deep hole he had dug for himself. But it was like trying to crawl out of the Grand Canyon. Albert Thews would admit later, "This was probably the most difficult case, from a legal standpoint, that I have ever tried."

By this point, he had to admit to the jury that all three slayings were probably committed because Gonzales was romantically obsessed with women who were unavailable to him. He then went on to say that Gonzales had indeed stabbed Barbara Muszalski with a kitchen knife. But he was looking for voluntary manslaughter charges, not first-degree murder.

Albert Thews said, "He did it in a white-hot rage. With that sudden rage came that stab-stab-stab, until he stopped and realized what he had done. He did it in a fit of passion that was not premeditated murder."

But Deputy D.A. Morris Jacobson had a very different take on Benjamin Pedro Gonzales. He told the jurors in his final argument, "He's a thrill killer. A criminal genius trying to beat a first-degree murder conviction. He's trying to defeat the concept of premeditation. He's telling you, 'I was high, I was an abused child, I was in a rage.' He became obsessed with women—co-workers who were romantically unavailable to him. When they rejected his advances, he stalked them and stabbed them. He didn't just have a bad night because they turned him down. He stews on it. He comes up with a murder plan. . . . The attacks are vicious. A big bloodbath."

Then Jacobson focused on how Gonzales managed to sneak the ten-inch kitchen knife into Barbara Muszalski's pickup. "There's no other way for that butcher knife to get into that truck. This defendant plans to have his rages. He fixates, he deliberates, he premeditates, and he mutilates."

On December 10, 1998, after all the years of delays and false starts, the jury came back with a decision in the case after only three hours of deliberation. When Judge Jeffrey Horner asked how they found the defendant, the foreperson said, "We, the jury, in the above mentioned case, find the defendant, Benjamin Gonzales, guilty of first-degree murder."

Fourteen

Charles Manson's Neighbor

On the date of sentencing, January 8, 1999, defense attorney Albert Thews was still trying to get Gonzales committed to a state hospital, rather than state prison, arguing that he was insane and unable to present a valid defense. Deputy D.A. Morris Jacobson strongly objected. He told Judge Horner, "You know the likelihood of his flight. I brought a lot of evidence to you about the kind of flight risk he is and how dangerous he is once he flees, how he changes his appearance and his name and blends in and disappears. The danger posed by his flight is extreme. Perhaps it's beyond extreme. He is a true serial killer. I can almost guarantee that if he walks out the door here, he will kill again. He may kill again while he is in custody. He's shown a lot of indications of that. And that under the standards in counsel's papers cannot be met. I object in the strongest possible terms."

The judge agreed with Jacobson's assessment, and he said, "I see no grounds presented to me, nor do I see any grounds in my own independent review of all the evidence presented in this case to indicate that the execution of the judgment—the passing of judgment and execution of judgment—should not take place today. This matter has been pending in court for seven years. There have been a number of proceedings, very lengthy, exhaustive proceedings ultimately, resulting in convictions that I briefly touched upon earlier. I feel that this is the place and time for judgment to be passed."

Before Judge Jeffrey Horner passed down judgment on Benjamin Gonzales, California law required the Victim Impact Statement, which gave the friends and family of Barbara Muszalski a chance to speak their piece.

Deputy D.A. Jacobson called Barbara Muszalski's daughter, Jamie Muszalski Heston, to the stand.

She said, "Judge, my mom was a wonderful, thoughtful, special woman. And she was an awesome mom. I remember once when she surprised me and brought me a cooler to my workplace that contained a box of minute rice and chop suey, one of my favorite homemade meals. For no reason, just because.

"One time I auditioned to be a vocalist for a band, and when I got it, she sent me a beautiful bouquet of flowers in an unusual vase that looked like two black-gloved hands poised to clap, as if to congratulate me on my accomplishment. Mom was thoughtful and creative, always anticipating the needs of those she loved.

"We talked on the phone every week, sometimes several times a week. We went out to lunch at least two or three times a month, chatting and gossiping like good friends. Many daughters might have had an adversarial relationship with their mothers, but not me. She was my best friend, my advisor, my confidant and my mother.

"Mom and Dad were so in love. I was unusual in that I had parents who were not divorced. And not only were they not divorced, they were happy. Mom mentioned many times that she couldn't wait until Dad retired so they could spend all their time together. They were very affectionate with each other, always. Then April 9, 1992, happened.

"When she was so violently ripped away from us, so many things changed. The ranch house where I thought my parents would live out their days, where I lived my teen and young adult years, now belonged to . . . belongs to a stranger. The farm animals Mom raised were all sold quite a long time ago. No more adorable baby goats to feed, no more roosters crowing, no more beautiful sunsets on lush green hills surrounding our home. The peaceful farm, the comings and goings, the parties, the friendships maintained by Mom, all gone.

"My father now lives two hours away from me, and I mostly see him on holidays. I have a stepson who will never know his grandmother. He will never be pleasantly surprised by her love and incredible generous spirit.

"Mom missed my wedding, one of the most important days of my life, and will miss the day when I bear my first child.

"I have a husband who will never experi-

ence the loving and very hip mother-in-law
that she would have been. My husband only
knows my mother through what I've told him,
not nearly enough for him to know the full
extent of what he's missing.

"I have forgotten so many things about her
life that she told me. Bless the times when
your relatives tell a story for the tenth time,
for at least you will never forget it.

"Recently my husband asked me to recall
something about Mom, and I couldn't. It was
something so simple that should have been in
my memory, but already, and only seven years
after her murder, my memory fades about
some details.

"I hate that I never learned to crochet, knit
and spin like she did. I hate that I never
picked up all the family recipes that were in
her head. I hate that when I need advice,
when I want to talk to her, I can't make a
simple phone call and do it. I thought I had
more time.

"The initial pain was overwhelming, all con-
suming, when I lost her. Over time, because
life goes on as always, the pain dulled, but is
immeasurable. So many little things that catch
me off guard. Perhaps a car that looks like
hers, a picture of her that I come across, or
I see a happy intact family to be jealous of.
Or perhaps I'm having a happy moment and
suddenly feeling it's a great loss because she
would have enjoyed being there for it. Immeasurable moments of pain.

"She touched me and made a difference in
hundreds of people's lives.

"My life on the surface has gone on. Perhaps to a stranger I have even prospered and done well for myself. But I would give it all back and more to have her here. A stranger will never know how many nights I weep, how many moments of stabbing pain I experience from the loss that affects me on a daily basis, even today, almost seven years later. You'll never know the pain, loss and emptiness I feel on every single family holiday, birthday, Mother's Day and anniversary of her death.

"When I want to visit Mom, I only have a cold grave to go to. It should not be this way. I should have a mother to call and talk with, share with, laugh with, and cry with. But I don't, and I never will.

"I don't get another chance. I don't get a reprieve. I don't get paroled from a sentence that was handed down to me on April 9, 1992. It was also handed down to my father, my brothers, my grandmother, my uncle, our friends and so many others. Our life sentence is life without the possibility of parole.

"And this evil monster, this sick, disgusting, unrepentant, vicious, morbid degenerate should receive no less than what I got, Judge. I implore you to impose the maximum sentence allowed."

No less poignant and searing was the Victim Impact Statement of Barbara's husband, Jim Muszalski. He said, "Your Honor, I've been kind of dreading this part of the justice process ever since I heard of it—the Victim Im-

pact Statement. How can you ever hope to
capture the utter despair of being a survivor
of a heinous crime?

"How can you people understand that a remarkable person had been senselessly lost to
the world?

"I wrote this in the morning—there it is 4:20
A.M. on another day that I can't return to sleep
after waking abruptly, thoughts of Barbara com-
manding my consciousness, demanding, seeking,
desperately hoping for an answer that doesn't
resolve the harsh truth of her violent death.
Some mornings I can concentrate on the good
things. Many mornings I concentrate on the
good things—her smiling face welcoming me
home after a long day of work, the ebb and
flow of people and animals defining another fulfilling day on the ranch, the quiet and tender
moments together at the end of the day, making
plans for our retirement, looking forward to our
children starting their own families and the anticipated joy of future grandchildren.

"Then there are days when I can't even get
to sleep without prescription drugs—anxiety
pills they're called—an occasional appointment with a peer counselor, all necessary to
survive another day. Even the pills refuse to
help; a strong feeling of panic rising in your
chest warning of something dangerous about
to happen; afraid to close your eyes, mind rac-
ing over everything and nothing in particular.
No threat that you can face and defeat, just
the emptiness of another day without Barbara.

"We've spent the last few months in trial
talking around Barbara, not seeing the loving

person that taught me how to be a loving father and husband, not reviewing the highlights of her life, the unselfishness in helping others, the nurturing presence, the intelligence, the compassion and unswerving love of life. Here was a foster mother to over twenty children, a resource to senior citizens and schoolchildren, a community volunteer and a respected livestock expert.

"Gone is the tranquillity and comfort of over thirty-five years of loving companionship, gone is the loving mother of our children, gone is the great grandmother to our future grandchildren, gone is my best friend. All gone.

"People ask, 'How are you doing?' I'm surviving is the usual answer. Just surviving.

"It's been over six years since Barbara's death. Finally, justice is being served. No more innocent women will die at the hands of this fiendish killer. My one desire is that he never be allowed to murder again, that he be kept behind bars for the remainder of his pitiful life. That will be the final tribute to Barbara and the kind of life that she led.

"In closing, I've got a few words from the song that means a lot to me over the last seven years. And it says:

What will I do with just a photograph to
    tell my troubles to?
When I'm alone with only dreams of you
    that won't come true
What will I do?

"It's something I face every day."

***

But if Jim Muszalski thought he would have
the last word, he didn't take into account Benjamin Gonzales perpetrating one more outrage
in court.

Defense attorney Albert Thews asked Gonzales, "Do you wish to address the court?"

Gonzales answered, "At first I didn't. But after the testimonies that I heard today from
family members and others, I think only . . .
I should say something.

"I feel like I owe Barb something, which I
think is a ridiculous statement. She was also a
very good friend to me; in fact, one of the
first people throughout my life, even through
childhood, who I confided in so much. And
she was a very good person. She helped me
when I was on the run. I confided in her everything that happened in my life. She showed
me understanding. She showed me a lot of
great care. She was always interested in me
and asked questions about my childhood, the
abuse from my father and this and that.

"I feel bad she had to meet some . . . somebody, with a boy so enraged, so abused, that
it's . . . I don't know how to explain, what to say.

"All my life's been . . . I hurt myself, in every
kind of way imaginable. I've been through so
many things in my life, and every situation I've
run upon, instead of trying to advance myself,
which I had many opportunities, I'd do something where I'd be hurt by others.

"Barb understood that . . . and I also think
of her on holidays, and also feel bad.

"I also remember the first time in my life that somebody really cared and understanded [*sic*]. When I was a child, when I used to go to people and tell them about my father and this and that, when I told men, a couple of the men wanted to sexually abuse me. When I told other people, they didn't want to hear it, or they would say something about my father. And I'd be tied to a pole and whipped again.

"She was the first person who ever listened to me, who ever cared, who ever asked me questions. I will also miss her. I feel bad she had to meet an enraged boy.

"I don't know what to say. I did not even plan on saying nothing. I feel real touched by what other people have said.

"I feel Barb was also in a . . . in . . . I don't know how to say it. She was happy in her life. But she was also disturbed. She felt she couldn't open up to people around her, so she came to strangers. I confided in her, and she confided in me. She had problems and I didn't understand. It was strange how it all started off. . . ."

By this point Deputy District Attorney Morris Jacobson had heard enough of Gonzales's self-serving diatribe. Every word he spoke was like a slap in the face to the Muszalski family.

Jacobson rose from his seat and said, "Your Honor, I'm going to interpose an objection at this time. Unless Mr. Gonzales wishes to address sentencing, I believe further recitation of his view of the victim and whether she deserved to die is inappropriate at this time."

Judge Horner replied, "Mr. Thews, do you wish to be heard?"

Albert Thews responded, "I submit the issue."

The judge turned toward Benjamin Gonzales and said, "Mr. Gonzales, why don't you approach the issue of sentence at this time."

Gonzales answered, "Okay, whatever you like, Your Honor. I committed suicide in court to be heard again. To feel something beyond the trial. So you know it will get past."

Finally it was time for Judge Jeffrey Horner to pronounce sentence upon Benjamin Pedro Gonzales, and he minced no words about it. He said, "Benjamin Gonzales is the single most dangerous individual presently housed in the Alameda County Jail and that he will most certainly be among the most dangerous inmates to be housed anywhere in the California State Prison System. The evidence in the lengthy trials and hearings in this case establishes beyond all doubt that Mr. Gonzales poses a clear, immediate and present danger to every single person with whom he comes in contact—prison staff, attorneys, transportation personnel and other inmates. Without question, he must continue to be housed in an isolated setting in the most secure facility which can be provided within the prison system. To do otherwise will be to put at risk of death—and I repeat, absolutely anyone—with whom Mr. Gonzales comes in contact.

"Mr. Gonzales is a vicious, sadistic, brutal serial murderer. I've been involved in the system of the Alameda County criminal justice system for thirty-three years. I have never come in contact with any person whom I believe combines the traits of sadistic brutality, viciousness, lack of remorse and depravity to the degree these traits are exhibited in Mr. Gonzales. He should serve every year, every week, every day, every minute of the sentence imposed by law. He should never be released on parole. Never!"

Then Judge Horner pronounced a sentence of thirty years to life in the highest maximum-security prison that California had to offer.

To which Benjamin Gonzales replied in a twisted and ironic quip, "Thank you, Your Honor. You sound just like my father."

After Judge Horner pronounced sentence, the authorities at Alameda's North County Jail were so eager to be rid of Gonzales that they shipped him straight to San Quentin Prison, rather than back for a stay at the county jail, as was the usual procedure. As Kathy Boyovich said, "He was treated like a death-penalty inmate."

Deputy D.A. Morris Jacobson summed up the general feeling when he told reporter David Holbrook of the *Contra Costa Times*, "He's a pro manipulator of the system with Houdini-like abilities and a thirst for blood."

But San Quentin was just a stopover for Benjamin Gonzales. He was ultimately bound for California's toughest prison—Corcoran State Prison. Even Lance Corcoran, vice-president of the California Correctional Officers Association, said, "Given there are 160,000 inmates in the state prison system, these are the worst of the worst."

He failed to add that Corcoran State Prison was also one of the most dangerous places in America. In the 1990's, the inmates not only had to watch out for the other inmates, they had to watch out for the guards as well. By the time Benjamin Gonzales was being shipped there, Corcoran State Prison had a reputation for incredible violence. It was a strange unit right from the start. It came about because Folsom State Prison and some of the other state prisons were exploding with gang violence by 1985. The authorities in Sacramento decided to put the worst inmates from all the state prisons in one place.

As the first warden, George Smith, said, "We were going to take the garbage from everybody else." And within Corcoran was built a maximum-security area for the worst of the worst—the Security Housing Unit [SHU], where the likes of Sirhan Sirhan, Charles Manson, a top leader of the Aryan Brotherhood, and mass-murderer Juan Corona were shipped. Into this volatile mix were added 1,500 other extremely dangerous inmates from rival gangs.

San Quentin Deputy Warden Lewis Fudge warned, "It is akin to forcing integration among the Catholics and Protestants of Northern Ireland."

To make matters worse, seventy percent of the incoming guards and staff were fresh out of the academy. After only six weeks of training, they were expected to deal on a daily basis with the worst of the Mexican Mafia, Aryan

Brotherhood, and the Crips and the Bloods. The highest authorities came up with a cock-eyed plan to mix the rival gangs in the exercise yard, reasoning that the rival gang members would have to get along once they were released back into society, so they might as well get started in prison. But the underlying theme that was never officially spoken was inmates who fought could be punished. If they fought too long, even when warned, they could be shot.

In its first year alone, Corcoran racked up an incredible 1,500 fights. This averaged out at one fight per inmate. Daniel McCarthy, the retired director of California Corrections, was incredulous. He said later, "The level of violence was absolutely the highest I have ever seen in any institution, anywhere in the country."

Someone who had firsthand knowledge of all the violence occurring at Corcoran was a guard in the Security Housing Unit named Roscoe Poindexter. At six foot, seven inches, and weighing 270 pounds, he had been an All-American basketball player at Cal State Long Beach and even drafted by the Boston Celtics. He later told a *Los Angeles Times* reporter about how newly arriving inmates were treated. He said, "We knew they were inmates who had done wrong. We'd place them in a chin hold, tell them to look skyward, and any flinch to the right or left was reason to take them down. And all the while we're yelling at them, 'Welcome to Corcoran SHU! This is a hands-on institution. You're in our house now. Whatever your life in prison was before, it's over. Welcome to hell.' "

He also told the *Los Angeles Times* reporter how troublesome prisoners were given "re-education." He would wrap his big hands around the inmate's neck and begin squeezing while another guard would yank on the man's testicles. Poindexter would then whisper to the inmate, "Now don't you go passing out on me, you hear?" He said they called the technique "the Deep Six." It was like taking a dive underwater and not coming up for air. "You give a prisoner only enough air to hear your message. It wasn't in the manual. It wasn't part of the official training. It was grandfathered into me by my sergeant and the sergeant before him. It was brutality, but we never left a mark. I'll be honest with you. I was known as the Bonecrusher. I was used as an intimidation factor. When brute force was needed to get an inmate to comply, they called me in."

Inmate Eddie Dillard told the *Los Angeles Times* reporter, "Prison guards are their own gang, with their peculiar language, and walk and code. They have that same characteristic as street gangs—the same silence."

By the mid-1990's, Dillard's assessment of the Corcoran guards as a gang of their own was more true than he might have suspected. On a day in 1995—known ever after as "Ninja Day"—scores of guards donned black ninja-like uniforms, wore masks and covered their identifying badges. They called a mock fire drill and rousted hundreds of half-naked inmates out onto a small patch of sunburned lawn under the hot sun. Then they proceeded to beat and kick them.

Ten days later, a group of especially vicious guards, known as the Sharks because of their penchant for sudden and violent attacks, ushered a busload of new inmates into the facility. As the inmates walked off the bus, the guards warmed up with football-like cheers. After the cheering, the Sharks got to work. Using fists, batons and combat boots, they beat and stomped the new arrivals into submission. It was a lesson none of the arriving prisoners would ever forget.

By the time Benjamin Pedro Gonzales arrived at Corcoran State Prison in 1999, the worst abuses by the guards were a thing of the past. The FBI now kept a close watch on the facility and the habit of placing separate antagonistic gangs in the same exercise yard was over. But Corcoran was still a very dangerous place. Designed for 3,000 inmates, it now held 5,300. Benjamin Gonzales had not lost any of his own violent nature. It took him only a couple of months to get into two fights with other inmates and get himself thrown into the Special Housing Unit.

Gonzales was given a cell in a unit adjacent to Charles Manson, which was designated the Protective Housing Unit. He was close enough to Manson so that they could observe each other's daily activities. One thing he couldn't have missed was Manson playing his guitar. Manson was still totally devoted to his music, and so were his followers on the outside. They were still putting together tracks for CD's based on Manson's music. According to his disciple, Sandra Good, Manson said, "My music is not music. It's a rap, a talk. Nothing I do over. I do it once from the soul in a trance. It's not entertainment. I'm not a clown or an actor. I'm not in trade, nor am I running for office. I'm a prophet calling out warnings of ATWA [Air, Trees, Water, Animals]. I'm authority from God. Here is the trouble. We come out with new. Others grab it and run, and make movies and TV shows with distorted bits and pieces of the real for money and approval and rock-and-roll stars. That cuts it off."

Whatever Benjamin Gonzales thought of Charles Manson's music, he kept it to himself. In fact, he pretty much kept to himself as usual, except when lashing out in a rage against some other prisoner. Like Manson, he created his own world in his mind. And just like Manson, he said things that others could not understand. Each seemed to be speaking in a language of his own devising.

In the same unit with Charles Manson were Sirhan Sirhan, and Juan Corona, who was convicted of killing twenty-five farm laborers in the 1960's. There were only forty-eight individuals in the entire Protective Housing Unit. Lance Corcoran told David Holbrook, "These guys are at risk because of the notoriety of their crimes or because they snitched. They might be a target of an inmate who wants to make a name for themselves."

In March 1999, when Gonzales was there, that's exactly what happened. A broken door adjoining the Security Housing Unit was discovered by inmates in Benjamin Gonzales's section. They burst through the door, and a full-scale riot was underway. They chased Juan Corona down and beat him, and smashed Charlie Manson's guitar. Gonzales for once wasn't directly involved in the mayhem. He seemed to like to pick fights on his own. He was never one who joined a crowd.

Lance Corcoran related, "When those guys broke in, Charlie dropped his guitar and ran."

Charlie Manson may have been middle-aged by this point, with a pot belly, but he outran the assailants. It took a full-scale team of guards to quell the disturbance. Once again Corcoran State Prison lived up to its reputation of violence.

In April 1999, Los Angeles Police Detective Frank Bolan got a surprise contact from someone he had wanted to convict for years. It was Benjamin Pedro Gonzales. The murder of Dondi Johnson had always stuck in Detective Bolan's craw, especially since Gonzales had skated on it because of a legal technicality. Now in April 1999, Gonzales said he had something he wanted to tell Detective Bolan about the murder of Dondi Johnson. He intimated that he wanted to confess to the killing and give him the details. He even hinted that he might talk about more murders.

Detective Bolan agreed to the meeting at Corcoran State Prison and found himself motoring up Interstate 5 from the sprawl of Los Angeles, through the rugged Tehachipi Mountains and down into the fertile great Central Valley of California. Once he turned off onto State Route 43, he was surrounded by cottonfields, cornfields and vineyards. It was a world away from the mean streets of Los Angeles with its drugs, prostitutes and gang-bangers.

Right smack in the middle of all the agriculture was the maximum security prison of Corcoran, with its razor wire and guard towers. It looked about as foreign to the pastoral scene as the prisoners did compared to the rural farm folk.

Detective Bolan was ushered into the Security Housing Unit for his meeting with Benjamin Pedro Gonzales. If he hoped for a straightforward accounting from a coherent and remorseful Benjamin Gonzales, he was sadly mistaken. Detective Bolan met with what so many other law enforcement officials had experienced so many times before from Gonzales. After having just driven 150 miles, he was greeted with utter intransigence and complete hostility.

Detective Bolan said later, "I tried to talk to Ben through the cell door, but he just yelled a whole bunch of profanities. Then Charlie [Manson] took up the cause. They were both yelling and hollering."

Benjamin Pedro Gonzales was playing his crazy mind games right down to the bitter end.